HOW TO FIND
THE HELP
YOU NEED

How to Find the Help You Need

Dr. Archibald D. Hart
& Dr. Timothy F. Hogan

ZondervanPublishingHouse
Grand Rapids, Michigan

A Division of HarperCollinsPublishers

How to Find the Help You Need
Copyright © 1996 by Archibald Hart and Timothy F. Hogan

Requests for information should be addressed to:

ZondervanPublishingHouse
Grand Rapids, Michigan 49530

Library of Congress Cataloging-in-Publication Data

Hart, Archibald, D.
    How to find the help you need /Archibald D. Hart and Timothy F. Hogan.
      p.   cm.
    Includes bibliographical references.
    ISBN: 0-310-20111-X
    1. Psychology and religion. 2. Psychotheraphy. 3. Spiritual direction.
  4. Pastoral counseling. I. Hogan, Timothy F., 1963– . II. Title.
BV51.H374   1996
253.5—dc20   95-45638
                                                   CIP

All Scripture quotations, unless otherwise indicated, are taken from the *Holy Bible: New International Version®*. NIV®. Copyright © 1973, 1978, 1984 by International Bible Society. Used by permission of Zondervan Publishing House. All rights reserved.

Interior design by Joe Vriend

Printed in the United States of America

---

96 97 98 99 00 01 02 /❖ DH/ 10 9 8 7 6 5 4 3 2 1

To our spouses, Kathleen and Karen,
for their tireless patience, support,
and understanding.

Contents

Acknowledgments

We are deeply indebted to the many people who supported the preparation of this manuscript. Drs. Marcia Gilroy and Patricia Siegel at the Children's Hospital of Michigan graciously provided time for research. Nova Hutchins was invaluable in her patient and enduring work of organizing and combining earlier drafts of this text.

This work grew in clarity and wisdom thanks to the helpful comments of many colleagues and friends, including Mary Hogan, O.S.M., Richard Ludlow, M.D., Brian Madvig, Ph.D., and Eileen Murthy. In particular, we would like to acknowledge the incomparable assistance of Lori Walburg and the fine editorial staff at Zondervan.

Finally, no amount of words could express our gratitude to our spouses, Kathleen and Karen, whose patience, love, and forbearance have been constant, despite our frequent absences over the past three years while putting this work together.

Preface

As the dean of a Christian graduate school of psychology, I (Dr. Hart) have been confronted far too often with the devastation suffered by men and women whose efforts to seek healing have resulted in far worse suffering.

The stories which have filled my office and awakened my telephone are as tragic as they are diverse: I have helplessly watched the tears fall from the eyes of young patients who were sexually exploited by their psychotherapists. I have held the trembling bodies of grieving parents whose pastors had advised them not to take their children for psychological treatment for mental illness, illness which later caused these children to take their own lives. Others have lugged into my office the heavy baggage created by bungling spiritual leaders whose inept use of popular psychology caused more suffering than was there to begin with.

I have seen hundreds of these cases in the thirty years I have been practicing as a Christian psychologist. And as each one of these hurting people left my office or hung up the telephone, my resolve to protect Christians from such poor help has been strengthened.

This book was written to be a hands-on, practical guide for people interested in finding both psychological and spiritual help. We have two specific aims. First, to equip Christians to better understand the potential benefits and dangers of psychology. Second, to stress the important role of spiritual direction in the healing process.

We write this book for two groups of people with whom we have had many long consultations. The first and most important group consists of those people who are considering seeking either psychological help, spiritual guidance, or some combination of the two. This book is designed to

- show you how to locate someone who will help you,

- show you how to avoid those who will cause worse problems,
- show you how to interview potential counselors and spiritual guides, and
- provide tips to help you get the most for your money.

We are also writing for those who are already receiving some form of help and wish to evaluate how appropriate or effective it is. This book will help you to

- evaluate the effectiveness of your spiritual leader or therapist,
- teach you how to address difficult issues which might be keeping you from growing,
- show you how to identify the signs of "toxic" therapy, and
- help you know when it is time to get out of therapy or end spiritual guidance.

Archibald D. Hart, Ph.D.
Pasadena, California
Timothy F. Hogan, Psy.D.
Detroit, Michigan

PART 1

How to Find the Help You Need

Chapter 1

When Do You Need Help?

Anna had a difficult time pinpointing when she started going downhill. She had always considered herself a happy, well-adjusted Christian. To others she was considered a model for the young women in the church: prayerful, easy-going, committed, and helpful.

So Anna herself could not understand how she could end up in the office of a psychologist. "I just do not enjoy life anymore," she began. "I'm always irritable and angry, and I don't know what I want to do with my life. Even praying doesn't work anymore. God just seems to be hiding from me in my darkest hour." Anna began to weep.

Anna felt as though life were playing a mean trick on her. Despite her efforts to eat right, exercise, and pray regularly, she could not concentrate on her work, felt edgy all of the time, and on one occasion could not stop herself from crying. "The funny thing is," she went on, "other than Pastor Dave, who made me come see you, nobody from my church has any idea how I feel. Somehow I can always manage to pretend I am okay when I am there."

Anna needed help. Her own efforts to pull herself out of her discomfort were not working. Even long talks with Pastor Dave and her best friend only helped a little bit.

A psychological evaluation revealed that Anna, like others on her mother's side of the family, suffered from depression. For five months, Anna worked with a therapist and Pastor Dave. This helped her learn more about the source of her depression, helped her learn to fight it effectively, and helped her understand how God was able to work in her depression to bring deep and inner healing. In short, reaching out for help turned out to be a tremendous blessing for Anna.

Who Needs Help?

Anna thankfully found help when she needed it. But how are you to know when you can benefit from outside help? If you were to listen to the advertisements for Christian counselors, you might conclude that *everyone needs help!* And in many places, this actually is the expectation! At my church in the Midwest, almost all of my (Dr. Hogan's) closest associates had some type of spiritual director; when I moved to California, almost all of my closest friends had a therapist!

However, not *everyone* should seek help every time he or she feels a little discomfort or suffers from some psychological symptom. Rather, by participating fully in the life of a Christian community, by remaining committed to healthy relationships with friends and family, and by pursuing the spiritual disciplines, many of life's changes and challenges naturally become times of growth.

But sometimes life becomes too difficult to handle, even with the support of good friends and family. In those times, you may need to get some form of help, be it psychological, spiritual, or both.

Opportunities for Growth

There are many times in life when the challenges we face provide us with an opportunity for growth. These opportunities are sometimes obvious and sometimes disguised. They may be staring us in the face and beating us over the head demanding attention, or they may be whispering to us through our feelings of emptiness.

If we seize the moment, recognizing these opportunities for growth, we can make a quantum leap in our spiritual and emotional maturity. Therefore, the first step is to identify and recognize those times when we are most ripe for growth and change.

What are those opportunities for growth? Allow us to suggest a few:

Times of Psychological or Spiritual Distress

The first opportunity for growth comes when we are in psychological or spiritual distress. Although this seems obvious, it is amazing how many people in trouble fail to get help for themselves—and miss an opportunity to grow. Such folks often go on to live a large part of their lives either licking their wounds or becoming numb or apathetic. Such people, regardless of their circumstances or the cause of their trouble, *should seek help*.

In case it is not clear what we mean by "psychological or spiritual distress," we refer you to Table 1. While this brief questionnaire is in no way a substitute for either a psychological or medical consultation, it should give you some idea of whether you need professional help. If you are in any doubt about what you should do or are seriously concerned about how you have scored on this test, begin by consulting your family physician.

Table 1
Signs of Psychological Distress

To assist you in determining whether you are in need of help at this time in your life, answer TRUE or FALSE to each of the following questions, as they apply to you during the past few months. Give yourself the number of points shown for each time you answer the question TRUE, and total up your score at the end.

Do you suffer from:

1. Difficulty falling asleep? (2 points)
2. Loss of appetite? (2 points)
3. Decreased interest or pleasure in doing things? (2 points)
4. Thoughts of killing yourself? (3 points)
5. Feeling down or depressed? (2 points)
6. Frequent headaches? (1 point)
7. Rapid heartbeat or pounding in your chest? (1 point)

8. Feelings of fatigue or loss of energy? (1 point)
9. Frequent stomachaches, back pain, or chest pains? (2 points)
10. Frequent indigestion, nausea, constipation, or diarrhea? (2 points)
11. Feeling "on edge" or nervous? (2 points)
12. Feelings of fear or panic? (3 points)
13. Addiction to alcohol or some other substance? (3 points)
14. Feelings of loneliness and difficulty making friends? (2 points)
15. Moods that interfere with your work? (2 points)
16. Urges to do something drastic, such as have an affair, get a divorce, or quit your job? (3 points)
17. Inability to pray? (2 points)
18. A secret habit, relationship, or sin that you can't get rid of? (3 points)
19. Feeling that people are out to get you? (3 points)

Total points for questions answered TRUE _____

The more questions you have answered true, the greater your psychological distress.

Score 6 or less: While this is well within normal range, if you answered questions 8, 9, or 10 true, you may have a physical problem, so consult a physician right away.

Score 7 to 12: You are showing some signs of distress that can be either physical or psychological. Your distress may be transitory, but if not consult a professional right away.

Score 13 to 19: You are showing moderate signs of distress and can certainly benefit from getting professional help.

Score 20 or over: Your distress is severe and needs urgent attention. Seek professional help *today*.

Times of Significant Life Transition and Change

A second opportunity for growth often comes during times of significant life transition and change. For example, the death of a loved one, a divorce (your own, your parents', or even a friend's), or a life-threatening illness can each be opportunities for growth because they demand change. Reaching out for help seems the natural thing to do.

Even positive life changes can be fertile grounds for personal and spiritual growth. Marriage, for example, is a major life transition that is best prepared for by some premarital counseling. Counseling helps to insure that people have faced up to their actions and decisions honestly and maturely—it is an opportunity for growth! The same holds true for people making career decisions, going off to college, or even facing retirement.

Times When We Are Aware of Our Limitations

A third opportunity for growth comes during times when we are acutely aware of our limitations: when we fail at a job, or bungle our relationship with our teenager. At these times we are forced to face up to our failings and realize that without God we are hopelessly inadequate. These moments "break" our stubborn wills, and if we are humble enough to realize that we are not perfect, we might even come out of this discovery the better for it.

Such times make us open to growth because we may become more willing to change our world views, reconsider our careers and the sort of friends we are keeping, and even reevaluate our relationship with God.

There is an old adage that "the human heart is the only thing that works better after it has been broken." This is true! Only we would add one qualification to this adage: Human hearts work better when their wounds are given the proper conditions to heal!

Times of Failure

A fourth opportunity for growth often comes during times of failure. About a year ago I (Dr. Hogan) had breakfast with a friend who was in crisis. He had joined his law firm with the hopes of becoming a partner. He "sold out" for this goal, working sixteen-hour days for more than eight years to try to reach the pinnacle of his career. Then the partners decided not to invite him into their ranks.

He was devastated. Everything he had worked for seemed to crumble before his eyes. He decided at that time to cut back his hours, spend more time with his family, and focus on his spiritual life. Now, one year later, he sees God's hand in the partners' decision. Their decision turned out to be a blessing for his life, his family, and his relationship with the Lord.

This ability to transcend his failure was facilitated by getting the right kind of help in a moment of crisis. My friend learned an important lesson: Failures are to grow by. Failures help us to grow stronger, more able to withstand the trials of life. And every apparent failure needs to be turned around by getting some help for it.

Times of Honestly Facing Our "Unfinished Business"

A fifth opportunity to grow comes when we honestly face up to our "unfinished business." For example, people who are frequently humiliated by their parents as children often grow up having a hard time with authority. These people are often aware that something is wrong with the way they react to authority, but they can't pinpoint the reason. They assume that is just the way they are. True? No, often there is some unfinished business that needs to be addressed and understood.

Honestly facing such unfinished business creates a wonderful opportunity for growth and healing. While we may experience some pain by exposing past hurts, uncovering hidden anger, or discovering cancerous resentments, the freedom and maturity that is gained is well worth the pain.

Times When Things Just Aren't Getting Better

Finally, an opportunity to grow comes when we realize that things just aren't getting better. Imagine a close friend severs his relationship with you. Your feelings are hurt, but you assume that "time heals all wounds." So you talk about it with another friend, pray about it, and journal about it, all the while expecting that your feelings will begin to dissipate and your memory of the friend who has dumped you will begin to fade. But it doesn't. A year passes and you still find yourself obsessed with your lost friendship. You continue to harbor anger and resentment, despite your numerous confessions and prayers which you hoped would help.

Emotional wounds that don't heal are like any physical wound. We get burned, and we have pain. However, physical wounds typically heal over time. Even though they often leave a scar, the pain eventually recedes. However, if a physical wound continues to cause pain several months after it was inflicted, the wise thing to do is to seek some help for it. The same is true for emotional wounds.

A Window of Opportunity

Perhaps reading this first chapter has given you some hope that getting help is just what you need. Perhaps you have recognized a "window of opportunity" for personal and spiritual growth in your own life.

When you actually decide to reach out for help, however, you may find yourself running into common obstacles. But take heart. Don't let yourself become discouraged. In the next chapters, we identify those obstacles and show how to best overcome them.

Chapter 2

Obstacles to Finding the Help You Need

"Deep down I always dreaded that this day might come." Bob lifted his head to look at me. His whole body appeared to be aching in despair. His wife had just walked out on him.

This tall, strapping man, sitting and sobbing in my living room, was nothing like the Bob I had had breakfast with the week before. Sure, he had always struggled with his "bad days," but today he was unconsolable.

"I honestly don't see a reason to go on living, Arch." Bob continued to mumble, looking down at the tears dripping on his shoes. "I mean it. She was the only good thing that had ever happened to me, and now she is gone."

Bob was stuck. He needed help. But he had no idea where to look for help. Should he go to a psychotherapist, or just see his pastor? Or should he just pray about it? What if he ended up with a secular counselor who didn't share his beliefs?

These questions played like a broken record in Bob's head. Confused and hurting, Bob, like so many people today, had no idea where to turn for help.

Rational Obstacles to Getting Help

Bob's dilemma was real. The fear and confusion he felt about getting help was legitimate. In fact, there are many rational obstacles that can prevent people like Bob from finding the help they need.

Here are some obstacles that stand in the way of our getting the help we need.

1. Finding help is complicated.

When Bob consulted the Yellow Pages he found fourteen pages of advertisements under the heading "psychotherapist"! Many professional groups call themselves "psychotherapists." The yellow pages include "psychiatrists," "psychologists," "social workers," "counselors," "marriage counselors," "analysts," "therapists," and "mental health specialists." There were almost as many degrees listed: Ph.D., M.D., Psy.D., Ed.D., D.O., M.F.C.C., C.P.C., M.S.W., A.C.S.W., and the list went on and on!

Why are there so many different types of professions and training if everyone just does "psychotherapy"? How was Bob supposed to know whom he should call for the help he needed when so many advertise their skills? And if he does choose someone, how will he know he's not going to a snake charmer or a fortune teller? Valid questions these days!

Things did not get easier when Bob thought about getting some type of spiritual counsel or guidance. When he first joined his church, the pastor had told him that he could always come talk to him. But Bob realized that his pastor was grossly overworked and underpaid, so he didn't feel he could burden the pastor with additional problems. Besides, the pastor used illustrations from his counseling in his sermons, and he didn't relish the idea of becoming next Sunday's gossip!

He also thought about calling his discipleship leader, one of the ministerial staff, or the office for spiritual formation that his church had recently started. But what training have these people had? Would they really be able to help? How would he be able to face them in the future when they knew all his secrets?

Finally, a friend suggested that he go to a local monastery and talk to one of the priests who was a specialist in "spiritual direction."

At least this would ensure confidentiality, but Bob felt a little uncomfortable going to a monastery. He'd never been near one before!

All this was very confusing and complicated, so Bob had done nothing. And he was about to lose his marriage as a consequence.

2. Getting therapy can cost a fortune.

While spiritual guidance is often free, psychotherapy can cost a fortune. For example, typical fees for a good psychotherapist are more than $80 per session. In some areas (where office costs are high) it can cost $130 to $150 per session. Bob wasn't sure that the help he could get from a psychotherapist was worth this much money.

3. Not all therapists are sensitive to spiritual matters.

Not all helpers understand or can effectively work with a person whose life is committed to Christ. Bob knows that his healing will be by grace, and that he will grow closer to Christ through his suffering. But how can a helper who does not have a personal relationship with Christ ever help him open up to Christ's healing?

4. Getting help can be dangerous.

Whenever people open their hearts, share their pain, and ask for guidance, their inner lives—their core values—are vulnerable to change. For example, research on the effects of therapy clearly suggests that people who enter psychotherapy often take on some of the values of their therapist. Bob learned this firsthand: His wife's psychotherapist encouraged her to walk out on him.

We should choose very carefully to whom we entrust our minds. Secular psychologists are among the most non-religious professionals in America and are, as a group, less committed to traditional values, beliefs, and religious affiliations than most Americans.[1]

What's more, even though a psychotherapist may claim to be a Christian, he or she may not be trained to work from a solid Christian framework or to deal with spiritual crises.

5. Church leaders may not be trained to help with psychological and emotional problems.

Bob had a long history of so-called "bad days." These bad times were, in all probability, indicative of a serious problem with depression. This depression may have been caused by a change in his blood chemisty, but chances are that Bob's pastor did not have the necessary training to diagnose this type of problem.

In short, many of Bob's fears of going for help are rational and well-founded. They are legitimate. And, as Bob learned from his wife's experience, choosing the wrong therapist can have devastating consequences. More than anything, Bob needs help to find an effective therapist or spiritual guide.

Irrational Obstacles to Getting Help

Bob has identified significant obstacles to getting help, and he is rightly confused by all the options available to him. However, as I listened to Bob, I also sensed several irrational, misguided, and groundless fears that impeded his ability to get help.

1. We hold erroneous Christian beliefs.

Like so many people today, Bob had picked up a lot of theological nonsense on his spiritual journey. He had heard sermons that told him that "Christ is sufficient for all human needs," meaning, of course, that anxiety and depression are simply the result of unrighteous and unholy living. As Bob considered calling a therapist he heard the voice of one preacher from his past ringing through his mind: "God helps those who help themselves . . . Psychology is worldly, and of the devil . . . you need salvation, not psychotherapy. Just commit yourself more fully to God and all your problems will go away!"

These beliefs are neither Scriptural nor rational. "God helps those who help themselves" is not in the Bible. Rather, the New Testament tells us that there are many different roles and ministries within the body of Christ. We are to depend on one another and bear one another's burdens (Galatians 6:2). This dependence on one another for healing, counsel, and spiritual discernment is Paul's model for what the body of Christ on this earth is supposed to be.

Many critics of psychology have no hesitation about going to a dentist for a bad tooth or a surgeon for appendicitis, even if these professionals are not Christian. The healing of the mind, since it involves beliefs and values, is much more susceptible to the influence of non-Christian thinking, so we advocate caution in seeking out non-Christian help. But Christian psychologists and other mental health professionals, when appropriately screened, are as legitimate and helpful as other doctors and healers.

2. We have a natural fear of self-discovery.

Bob feared the uncovering of some of his deepest, darkest, secrets. He feared that talking about his early life might require him to recall painful memories or face dark and painful truths about his past, things he had worked hard to forget. Also, he feared finding out things about himself that he would rather not know.

This fear is common to many people who go for help. People fear the truth—especially about themselves. They lie to themselves for so long that they conceal the real truth about their inner lives.

But there is a remedy for such fear: The perfect love of Christ. What Bob will learn as soon as he becomes honest about himself is that "perfect love casts out all fear" (1 John 4:18). Bob will learn that because he has covered up his deepest secrets, he has been forced to live in deception. Facing up to the innermost parts of his past will help him to walk in the light of real truth. God's presence in the process will see to this. The energy he has been using for many years to guard the lies and secrets in his life can then be used to care for others and to live more fully himself.

3. We fear the opening up of old, painful wounds.

Like many of us, Bob has managed to cover up much of the pain of his childhood. He has a lot of unfinished business which he just has not dealt with. The mind is very much like the body. If an infection on the skin remains unhealed, several layers of skin will eventually grow over to cover and "protect" it. The infection is still there but hidden. In the same way, the mind likes to forget that so much unfinished business remains yet to be resolved, but if anyone gets close to the problem, it is very sensitive and painful.

Bob knows that the healing of these covered wounds might be painful because they must first be exposed. Bob's fear makes sense! Going for help will likely be upsetting. The infection must be lanced and drained. Before the healing can come, he will experience pain. But once the hurt is exposed, it will begin to heal, and he will be more healthy than he has been in a very long time. As with physical wounds, psychological wounds respond best to a little sunlight.

4. We fear we will lose control and go crazy.

Bob fears the power of the feelings he has blocked off over the years. He senses a great deal of power pent up in the unknown of his unconscious. After thinking about his pain, he finds himself daydreaming about "falling apart" or "losing it." On more than one occasion he has shaken his head and said, "If people really knew me, they would find out that I am crazy—that I am defective and unacceptable."

Many people experience the fear of going "crazy" when they first enter psychotherapy. We hear it all the time from people who come to our office. However, this fear is irrational. It is the last-ditch effort of the emotional defenses to keep you from becoming healthy. Rather than "losing" their sanity, people who face their difficulties honestly often find that they gain a great deal of sanity. In fact, the surest sign that a person is not losing his sanity is that he fears losing it! Those who become psychotic usually don't have such fears.

5. We fear that going for help is a sign of weakness.

We often fear that going for help is a sign of defeat, weakness, or lack of toughness. Bob often whispers to himself, "I should be able to handle this by myself. I shouldn't have to rely on anyone else to get me through. Going for help is for weak people, and I am not a weak person." But seeking help is not a sign of weakness; it is a sign of strength. It takes a strong person to admit that he or she needs help.

In our culture there is no stigma about going to a physician or dentist when we have physical pain. But emotional pain has its stigma. Emotional or even spiritual crises are considered a sign of weakness. Going for help publicizes this weakness.

Our culture's approach to mental health is still plagued by this irrational fear. Consider the consequences if we were to take the same approach to physical health. What if only those with chronic or life-threatening physical illnesses went to see their doctor? We would skip immunizations, physicals, heart evaluations, and all forms of early diagnosis and intervention. We all know what would happen: The hospitals would be jammed with people receiving treatment for preventable illnesses! In many ways this is precisely the case regarding emotional problems. Because we ignore or downplay warning signs of emotional illness, we end up with even worse problems—as Bob himself discovered.

Conclusion

Any of these fears—rational or irrational—can prevent us from finding the help that we need. The goal of this book is to move you past those fears, to point you toward the person who is best equipped to help you, and to start you on a journey toward wholeness and health.

But what is the *goal* of healing and growth? To put it bluntly and honestly, there is no point embarking on a journey toward healing if you are not clear about the destination!

The next chapter will make clear what that goal is. Don't skip it, for it is vital to understanding what the rest of this book is all about.

Chapter 3

Establishing Your Goal: Building Christian Character

Kay is a single mother of three children. She came to my (Dr. Hogan's) office after her husband left her unexpectedly for another woman. Kay was burdened with her own anger and anguish for her children. Yet somehow, in the midst of all her pain and confusion, Kay started every day with her arms outstretched before God, pouring out her hurt and anger, and waiting on God to give her the strength to go on. She maintained a regular exercise program, read inspirational books, and stayed in close contact with her Christian friends and pastor. She told me that she was doing all this in an effort to face her pain honestly and to open herself to healing.

Kay exemplifies Christian character. Her core identity—her heart, mind, soul, and strength—is centered in Christ. Her sole purpose in life is to embody the character of Christ in every part of her being.

Often the goal of psychological change is short-term. People seek cures for their depression, their phobias, their addictions, or their dysfunctional relationships. Once those problems are supposedly fixed, they believe they've reached their goal.

We, however, would like to propose a loftier goal. A far-reaching goal. A goal to strive for the rest of your life. That goal is the formation of Christian character.

Understanding Christian Character

If you were to look up the word *character* in a dictionary you would discover that it refers mainly to what something is made of and what it does. Etymologically, the word *character* comes from the Greek root *charassein,* meaning "engrave." This is about as perfect a definition as we can think of. Christian character means that our beings are "engraved" with the character of God. His character is so indelibly inscribed in our persons that it cannot be rinsed off!

Moses sums up well the goal of Christian character—as well as the process by which we are "stamped" with God's mark:

> "Hear, O Israel: The LORD our God, the LORD is one. Love the LORD your God with all your heart and with all your soul and with all your strength. These commandments that I give you today are to be upon your hearts. Impress them on your children. Talk about them when you sit at home and when you walk along the road, when you lie down and when you get up. Tie them as symbols on your hands and bind them on your foreheads. Write them on the doorframes of your houses and on your gates" (Deuteronomy 6:4–9).

What powerful images of character formation are expressed here: *impress* the commandments on your children; *talk* about them; *tie* them; *bind* them; *write* them! These are the ways we develop Christian character in ourselves: we let God permanently *burn* his character into our being.

In Mark 12:29–30, Jesus reiterates and updates this goal of Christian character formation. When a teacher of the law asks Jesus which is the most important commandment, Jesus replies:

> "The most important one . . . is this: 'Hear, O Israel, the Lord our God, the Lord is one. Love the Lord your God with all your heart and with all your soul and with all your mind and with all your strength.' The second is this: 'Love your neighbor as yourself.' There is no commandment greater than these."

Together, these texts paint a clear picture of what it means to have Christian character: It means that our relationship with God must ultimately involve our whole person—mind, heart, soul, body, and relationships. We cannot have Christian character in just one part of us! What is more, by encompassing our total being in a relationship with God through Christ, we experience healing, direction, and growth in all dimensions of our lives. To be a person of Christian character, therefore, we must

- love God with all our *heart,* allowing Christ to heal our emotional pain and freeing us to love and experience the joy of God;
- love God with all our *soul,* by committing ourselves to spiritual growth;
- love God with all our *mind,* seeking to take on the mind of Christ in all things;
- love God with all our *bodily strength*, acknowledging that our bodies are temples of the Holy Spirit;
- love God by loving our neighbor, thereby acknowledging God's presence in our relationships.

Many people make the mistake of seeing the spiritual dimension of Christian character as just one part of our total being. In this view, Christianity affects only the "soul" or "spirit," but has nothing to say about our minds, bodies, emotions, or relationships. Figure 1 summarizes this compartmentalized view of Christianity.

Figure 1
A Model for Christian Character

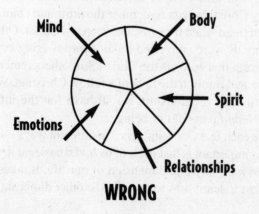

In our view, however, "spirit" is at the center of our minds, bodies, emotions, and relationships. How we view those areas directly affects our spiritual relationship with God. Figure 2 demonstrates how our spiritual life, in Christ, is at the center of our being.

Figure 2
Model of Christian Character

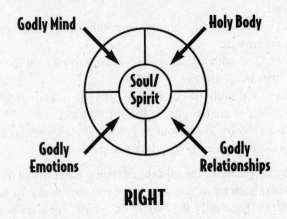

The Dangers of a Lopsided Christian Character

As you reflect on your walk with Christ, you will recognize the different ways in which Christ has touched each dimension of your being. Many Christians can remember the profound emotional way God touched them when they first encountered Christ. Others recall how their minds were converted by an overpowering comprehension of the truth that Jesus is the Christ. Still others remember how God became real through the love of a fellow Christian. Whether in emotion, mind, or relationship, we all have felt the influence of Christ in different parts of our being.

Why we each feel God's influence in different ways is not important. What is important is that most of us find it easier at first to allow Christ to work in only one dimension of our life. It takes time and directed effort to learn how to grow in the other dimensions.

For instance, some Christians find it easier to develop their intellect first. Other Christians are more comfortable developing their emotions. An Episcopalian professor may look with distrust upon an emotional Pentecostal, while that same Pentecostal may think the Episcopalian's faith is dead without emotional expression. Our church backgrounds, race, gender, and personality all help us to determine what aspect we are most comfortable developing.

The problems begin when we emphasize one aspect of ourselves at the expense of the others. For example, mind-oriented people might try to deny, suppress, or disown feelings—to their own detriment. Or emotions-oriented people may devalue the mind when they discourage higher education and critical thinking skills.

God must really grieve at this compartmentalizing of his wonderful creation. He has given us a mind and body, a head and heart, and unless we are able to express every aspect of our being, in both worship and service, we are not totally healthy.

If we devalue any aspect of our total being and overdevelop another, we may prevent ourselves from developing a genuine and balanced Christian character. We become lopsided, unstable, and a discredit to the gospel we purport to follow.

When I (Dr. Hart) first came to Christ at age seventeen, several of my buddies were also saved. Together we started on a journey of spiritual growth. Some of my buddies got caught up in a very emotionally driven form of worship. They had a great time "experiencing" their faith, but didn't receive a lot of food for their minds. I, on the other hand, became a lay preacher and started in on some meaty theology. I had had a very profound conversion, but I realized that I needed to understand the basis of my faith or else my feelings would rule the day. As I soon discovered, feelings are fickle and can't be trusted to last. Every one of my buddies, within just a few years, had abandoned their faith. The reason? Their emotions burned out!

Is your Christian character balanced? Is it healthy? Does it reflect the influence of Christ on your total being? The next section of this book will help you evaluate the current state of your Christian character by focusing on the five areas of our being: our minds, souls, bodies, hearts, and relationships.

Developing Christian Minds

Growing in Christian character demands that we learn how to think with the mind of Christ. The call to form our minds in the ways of God echoes throughout both the New and Old Testaments. Moses directed God's people to *learn* and *know* God's commandments (Deut. 6:1–15). Paul told the people of Rome, "Be transformed by the renewing of your mind" (Rom. 12:2), and he prayed that the love of the people of Philippi would abound "in knowledge and depth of insight" (Phil. 1:9). We cannot grow spiritually if we neglect our minds.

In short, a mind marked by Christian character (1) establishes godly assumptions and (2) practices Christlike thinking.

1. Establishing godly assumptions

James Allen, in his little but well-known book *As a Man Thinketh,* wrote: "Character is the sum total of all your thoughts." He then goes on to show that our every act springs from the hidden seeds of thought. How we think determines what sort of person we are.

Faulty thinking can hamper Christian character-building in many ways. One is to hold on to *false assumptions.* Assumptions are those beliefs we don't think to question because we take them for granted. For example, many of us believe that we are entitled to blessings from God based solely upon our behavior. "I go to church every Sunday, so why doesn't God give me what I ask for?"

This idea is based on a distorted form of cause-and-effect thinking: "If I do such-and-such, then this will happen." Spiritually, such thinking can get us into a lot of trouble. Sometimes we must do the right thing even if we do not see its effect.

A more biblically correct way of thinking would be not to emphasize rewards or payoffs in return for being good, which is what cause-and-effect thinking tends to foster. We should give priority to being faithful and obedient simply because we are grateful to God and he commands it. Such thinking opens us to a deeper experience of God's presence during times of suffering or long periods of unrewarding labor.

2. Practicing Christlike thinking

Christlike thinking does not come about automatically. Rather, it has to be practiced. Every day we are faced with having to make difficult decisions about how and where God is working and leading us. Such decisions require more than a mind that knows a lot of facts and Bible verses. The mind marked by Christian character thinks critically *and* exercises discernment.

But sometimes we neglect to use our minds, pretending such behavior is Christian. For instance, we look for a "sign" from God, rather than exercising our faith and mind. We want God to short-circuit our thinking capacity and just give us simple and quick answers. But this isn't always God's way. He wants us to apply godly thinking to our problems and thus shape our character to be more like his.

Developing Christian Souls

The development of Christian character is brought together and grounded in the development and growth of our spiritual center, the soul. The soul is the center of our being, the deepest part of us that comes to life when we are praying. Strong Christian character can only be built on the foundation of a healthy Christian soul.

To nourish our souls, we can do three things. First, we must take the health of the soul seriously. While our culture often acts as if the soul doesn't exist, Jesus taught that the soul is the source of all life. He warned, "Do not be afraid of those who kill the body but cannot kill the soul. Rather, be afraid of the One who can destroy both soul and body in hell" (Matthew 10:28).

Second, we must commit ourselves to an active prayer life. Just as we nourish the physical life of the body with healthy food, so do we nourish the spiritual life of the soul with genuine prayer.

Third, we must practice spiritual disciplines, such as reading and meditating on Scripture, keeping a spiritual journal, fasting, worshiping with fellow Christians, and serving in some form: teaching, helping, serving, leading, discipling, encouraging, and so forth.

When we are spiritually growing and our soul is healthy, we will face the challenge of building Christian character with clarity and enthusiasm.

Developing Christian Bodies

Perhaps the most neglected aspect of Christian character formation revolves around how we treat our bodies. Often, we give the body a very low priority in spiritual formation. Sure, we watch our weight, work out, jog, and consume vast quantities of vitamins, but our motivation is often self-preservation, not our growth as healthy Christians. Few really understand how the body figures into their spiritual well-being.

To grow in Christian character, we must treat our bodies as gifts from God. Our bodies enable us to follow Christ and participate in building his kingdom. We must understand four truths about our bodies if we wish to develop our Christian character:

1. We should love God with all our bodily strength (Mark 12:30). If we are to love God fully, we must pay attention to how we use our bodies and make efforts to keep them rested, well-nourished, and healthy.

2. We are the work of God's hands (Isaiah 64:8). God is the artist; we are his work of art. Our bodies are a part of his handiwork.

3. Our bodies are the temples of the Holy Spirit (1 Corinthians 3:16; 6:19). This is a wonderful thought. God does not dwell in our church buildings or cathedrals. He dwells in us!

4. Our bodies are central to God's work. God uses human hands, feet, minds, energy, and sweat to perform his purposes in the world (Isaiah 52:7; Acts 8:18). He uses our hands to feed the hungry and give water to the thirsty. What a humbling thought!

Our bodies are crucial, and if we abuse or neglect them, our relationship with God and others will suffer as a result. For example, if we push ourselves too hard, we may bring on stress-related illnesses that hamper our ability to work at all! Or if we choose fatty foods, we may suffer a heart attack. Even lack of a good night's rest can adversely affect our behavior.

So we can see that a healthy and well-kept body is essential to a full life. Even if we suffer from some chronic illness, we still have ways we can care for our bodies to minimize the effects of the illness. It is our spiritual responsibility to maintain our bodies.

Developing Christian Hearts

Building Christian character also means developing our hearts—the core of our emotions and center of our being. Feelings are an important part of who we are. Often God speaks to us in ways which are clearly not ideas or concepts, yet we recognize God's voice by the strong feelings that accompany it.

In order to distinguish God's voice, he must first heal our hearts. If our emotions are troubled, we are more likely to misread them—and what God is trying to say to us. The healing of the emotions is, therefore, an important aspect of the development of Christian character. Regrettably, this healing can often get blocked by psychological and emotional scars.

Often these emotional scars come from the painful experiences of childhood. Take, for example, the abandonment experienced by children of divorce. It can create a distrust of those who say they love us. These emotional scars can cause many problems with our relationship with God. Consequently, growing in Christian character often requires that we learn to face these emotional difficulties honestly and open ourselves to God's healing.

Developing Christian Relationships

Building Christian character also means that we allow our relationships to be formed and transformed by godly love: We are to love our neighbors as ourselves (Mark 12:31). God created people to need one another in order to survive. Relationships are not some extra bonus of the human condition to which we can have a "take it or leave it" attitude. Rather, people are designed to have relationships with one another.

Scriptures proclaim this need for relationships from beginning to end. God created humanity in pairs, because "it is not good for the man to be alone" (Genesis 2:18). And Christ not only told us to love one another but also declared that wherever two or three of us were gathered in his name, there he will be (Matthew 18:20).

Reaching out to love one's neighbor usually carries with it the very real risk of getting hurt. People abuse our trust. They move away. And they die. These emotional injuries can cause our hearts to harden and handicap our ability to relate with others. Consequently, growing in Christian character means that we face such painful experiences directly, so that our hurts can be healed by God, allowing us to continue to grow in love for our neighbor.

The Adventure of Building Christian Character

Since none of us are perfect, we are all "works in progress." To be human is to make mistakes. There is no perfection this side of heaven! As you have been reading this chapter, you have, most likely, become aware of the need for growth and the development of your Christian character. You might even have gained a sense of where and how God is calling you to more wholeness and health. But desiring to grow and actually growing are two very different things. What, then, is the secret to overcoming our weaknesses and in so doing building up our Christian character?

Paul frequently refers to this as "the work of Christ" and points us to this process in his letter to the Romans:

> And we rejoice in the hope of the glory of God. Not only so, but we also rejoice in our sufferings, because we know that suffering produces perseverance; perseverance, character; and character, hope. And hope does not disappoint us, because God has poured out his love into our hearts by the Holy Spirit, whom he has given us. (Romans 5:2–5)

Paul is telling us that how we handle suffering is a very important component of character formation. When the world breaks our heart, we need to turn to God to heal it. When we are confused and lose our way, we must turn to Christ to renew our minds.

We need not fear suffering. We need not dodge grief or sadness. When we cooperate with our suffering, it brings growth and a deeper healing experience. Through these ordeals we can expect to grow in the character of Christ. We do not seek them for the sake of growth, but we receive them as opportunities for the glory of God to be revealed (see John 9).

Thus Christian character is built not solely by our own effort or our own efficacy, but by the healing of Christ. Our job is simply to participate and cooperate!

Is this easier said than done? Of course it is. Participation in character formation is no easy matter. And the temptation to run away from the process is strong.

The Temptation to Shrink from Character Formation

When faced with our imperfections, physical problems, past mistakes, or unsatisfied longings, many of us become crushed and give up at the earliest opportunity. We resign ourselves to a life marked by vocational frustration, bad relationships, and perpetual melancholy. We go the way of the weak and retreat into fantasy in an effort to numb the pain. As a result, we become far less than what God created us to be. We shrink from the challenges that could actually strengthen our Christian character.

What are some ways we shrink from the tough work of character building?

1. We confuse our own problems with real suffering.

As believers we must accept suffering as an eventual and inevitable fact of life. The Christian way is the way of the cross! However, not all suffering is the same. Some suffering produces character; other suffering does not. Some suffering is noble, while other suffering comes simply as a consequence of our own foolishness.

For example, some people never save. They spend their money as fast as they earn it. When they find themselves in a desperate financial crisis, they bemoan their terrible predicament and complain about how God has let them down. Has he? Of course not! Reaping what one has sown is not the same as noble suffering.

If you discover that your suffering is largely a result of your own poor choices, you need to make changes. You need to grow in character, and God will bless you in that effort. But if you attempt to pin the blame for your problems on God, or your boss, or your spouse—watch out! You will only find yourself mired in even more problems.

2. We invest our energy in pursuing the wrong accomplishments.

Busyness can be a blessing when we need to distract ourselves from undeserved pain. But when we pursue busyness to block out pain, we deprive ourselves of the best opportunities for growth. Activity, even religious activity, does not form Christian character, yet many believe that if only they do more, they will become better Christians.

There is a story of a man who was searching under a streetlight for his keys. A woman approached him and asked, "What are you looking for? Perhaps I can help you find it."

"I lost my keys," the man replied.

"Where were you when you dropped them?"

"Oh, behind the building over there."

Puzzled, the woman asked, "Then why are you looking over here?"

The man sighed, "Because the light is better here!"

We laugh at this man's foolishness. But many of us are like him. We look for the fulfillment we desperately need in the most lighted, most convenient, or even the most available places. Sometimes we stay "under the light" just because it is the familiar place, the place that makes no demands and imposes no challenges. For example, many faithful and active church members are no longer growing in Christian character because they have remained involved with the same ministry for eons, even though it doesn't inspire them or bear fruit.

The challenge to grow in Christian character calls us to move out to unfamiliar places, to challenging and growth-producing ground. It calls us to replace our busyness with meaningfulness. If we are going to grow in Christian character we must move away from the well-lit and safe areas of our lives to the unfamiliar. It may be dark there, but God will meet us in our darkness if we trust him!

3. We fear making a mistake.

Many of us are deathly afraid of making a mistake. So we avoid taking risks, stifle our creativity, and grow bored and boring. We believe that being good or having a Christian image is more important than trying something new. We become like the person in the parable who buried his talent out of fear of making a mistake (Matthew 25:24–29). When he was finally called to account, he was told that he was a "wicked and slothful servant," and his talent was taken away and given to the man who had taken the greater risk. Life has no power for those who bury their talents. They are not broken and healed, a process which is essential to building Christian character. Their relationships are marked by low risk, shallowness, and a morbid fear of mistakes.

Building character is not passive but active! The person who actively works on building Christian character does not wallow in mistakes but turns them into building blocks. While she knows only too well the reality of human weakness, she knows even better, and gains strength from, the character of Christ. She can act boldly even in the midst of paradox, confusion, pain, and the very real possibility of offending some and shocking others.

Conclusion

So what does Christian character have to do with getting help? Simply this: Make sure that the help you get engraves God's character in your life. Ensure that every dimension of your person—including your mind, heart, body, and relationships—is affected. Don't settle for a "cure," an easier life, or a more prosperous existence. Instead, make your goal the building of your Christian character.

Now that you have your goal firmly in mind, let's turn back to our original question: "How do I find the help I need?" Because in our culture psychology is more familiar, let us turn first to the area of psychological help.

PART 2

Psychology and Psychotherapy

Chapter 4

Psychology in the Formation of Christian Character

We recently had lunch with a group of pastors who wanted to know how psychology and psychotherapy could benefit the people in their churches. They came prepared with several important questions, such as:

"What do psychologists have to offer Christians?"

"How can you tell if someone needs a psychologist?"

"Why do we suddenly need psychology in the church now? We didn't in the past. Isn't Jesus enough?"

These pastors were asking extremely important questions about the role of psychology and psychotherapy in forming Christian character. This chapter will address each of these questions in turn.

What Do Psychologists Have to Offer?

Psychologists offer two services which are often a valuable ministry in the church. First, they are good at psychological evaluation and intervention. This means that they are good at helping to identify and describe how people think, feel, and behave, and, more importantly, why they behave as they do. They are then able to use that information to solve problems and help people change in desirable ways.

Let us take a brief look at both psychological evaluations and interventions to understand how they might help us develop Christian character.

Psychological Evaluations

We live in a quick-fix culture with an insatiable appetite for instant anything! We love to get rid of anything that causes pain, gets in the way, or makes life more difficult—and we like to get rid of it fast! We don't want to really understand our problems. We just want to get rid of them.

I recently had a slow leak in one of my tires. When I took it to my dealership, the head mechanic told me that I wasn't the only one. "We've had all kinds of folks come in with them aluminum sport wheels with rim leaks. No problem, I'll have it fixed for you in twenty minutes." Quickly, he resealed my tire, took my money, and sent me on my way.

The next morning my tire was flat again. So I took it to a different mechanic. He, too, told me about the problem with "them aluminum sport wheels" and said there was an easy way to fix the problem, and proceeded to grind my rim and reseal my tire.

When I found the tire flat yet again the following morning, I took it to a third mechanic. This man was older and wiser and took much more time than the first two mechanics. When I told him that I had heard of the problem with "them aluminum sport wheels" he kindly nodded, then proceeded to methodically evaluate the tire, using different tools at each stage of the evaluation. He eventually discovered a nail embedded deeply within my tire, patched the hole, and sent me on my way.

Rather than having a trendy new problem with "them aluminum sport wheels," I had an old-fashioned, boring, nail-in-the-tire type of problem. But it took a careful diagnosis to get to the truth!

If we are honest with ourselves, we have to admit that we often want to do things just like the first two mechanics. We realize that we have a problem. We then remember a talk show, a popular book we've read, or the most recent sermon we've heard. We usually conclude that we have the most recent, common, or popular psychological problem advertised. Before we know it, we have bought three new books on the topic and joined a self-help group—all this *before* we have received a careful diagnosis.

Getting a psychological evaluation is like going to the third mechanic first. Psychological evaluations help us objectively understand our problems, as well as our strengths, weaknesses, and gifts. They can also help us to determine where we need to grow.

There are at least five types of psychological evaluations available, each of which helps to increase our understanding of how we function.

Intellectual Assessment: Intellectual assessments give an estimate of an individual's thinking abilities. In particular, it can tell what a person's strengths and weaknesses are. For example, while some people do well on tasks which require a lot of reading and language use, others do better on tasks like puzzles and nonverbal skills. When summarized and expressed in numbers, this is often called an "IQ."

Emotional Assessment: This type of assessment helps people to understand how severe their symptoms are and if they will need help to recover. For example, some people who say they feel depressed are really just sad in response to some life event and will likely recover quickly. Others, however, may have a biological depression and will need psychotherapy and sometimes medication to improve.

Neuropsychological Assessment: This type of assessment carefully assesses how well the various abilities of the brain and nervous system are working. It can tell what skills have been lost and which remain intact. For example, a neuropsychological assessment tells exactly which ways the memory works well and in which ways it may be weak. This type of assessment is particularly helpful after the brain has been damaged, either from the inside (e.g., a brain tumor or Alzheimer's disease), or from the outside (e.g., from a car accident).

Personality Assessment: This type of assessment helps people gauge what they are like. Personality assessments can determine whether a person is introverted or extroverted, organized or spontaneous, intuitive or experiential, and emotional or rational. They can also spot a tendency toward depression or anxiety. This type of assessment is often very helpful for those who are preparing for the ministry, or as part of a vocational assessment.

Vocational Assessment: This type of assessment helps people understand how natural talents, abilities, skills, and preferences prepare them for particular vocations and careers. One can also learn from this type of assessment what type of work would likely be most satisfying. Most people get some form of a vocational assessment from their high school or college counselor. However, as more and more people change careers later in life, they are finding this type of assessment helpful as they prepare for second and third careers.

Most psychological assessments use a combination of each of these five forms of assessment. Information from these assessments helps to assess strengths and weaknesses. This information, in turn, equips people with the tools they need to effectively develop Christian character.

Psychological Interventions

How easily do people change? Not very easily! Getting human beings to change has long been recognized as a difficult enterprise. Take the apostle Paul as an example. He admits quite openly that even though he always knew what he wanted to do, he still at times did the opposite (see Romans 7:15–25).

The difficulty people have changing their behavior was illustrated for me (Dr. Hogan) while I was working for a major cancer research hospital on the West Coast. This was a place where people were not only *aware* of the causes of cancer, but had *discovered* many of them. For this reason it was shocking to find, at any given time, a half dozen of these researchers standing outside of their research laboratories—the very laboratories where they discover causes for cancer—in their white lab coats smoking cigarettes!

Despite how difficult it is for people to change old habits and problem behaviors, the use of scientific psychological techniques are frequently very effective. Most forms of psychological treatment attempt to change people by focusing on one of four areas:

thoughts, feelings, behaviors, or relationships.[1] For each of these areas, it is assumed that change in one area will lead to a change in the other three. We limit our discussion here to the four approaches used by therapists which have proven to be most effective.

Changing Thoughts: *Cognitive therapy*. Cognitive therapists are very interested in the way we think about the world, and how thinking causes feelings and behaviors. Therefore, cognitive therapy helps to uncover irrational (or unbiblical) assumptions which underlie problems. Cognitive therapists teach effective and adaptive thinking skills, rather than spend too much time delving into early childhood memories searching for explanations that are at best only theories about how a problem may have started. Cognitive therapy usually helps feelings and behaviors to change by helping clients modify how they think about the world.

Changing Feelings: *Psychoanalysis and Psychodynamic therapy*. Psychoanalysis is one of the earliest forms of treatment and was promoted by Sigmund Freud, the "father of psychoanalysis." It is very different from most other forms of treatment in that (1) patients typically meet with their "analyst" three to five times per week, (2) patients lie on a couch and rarely look at their analyst, and (3) the focus of treatment is almost entirely on how the past influences the present.

While closely related in theory to psychoanalysis, psychodynamic therapy is very different in practice. Psychodynamic therapy encompasses a broad range of therapies that try to modify motives and drives. Here the therapist helps clients understand the underlying unresolved emotional conflicts in their lives. Therefore, psychodynamic therapists help clients reconsider and/or reexperience earlier relationships so that they can get insight into patterns of feeling which have become problematic. Dynamic therapists put great emphasis on the emotional relationship between the therapist and client and use it to expose how and why certain feelings arise.

Changing Behaviors: *Behaviorism*. Behavioral therapy simplifies problems to their simplest form. Behavior therapists look for the cause-and-effect relationship in a problem area. Instead of spending time on the inner workings of the mind, they focus on changing the basic behaviors that give rise to problems. Behavior therapists focus on the ways behaviors are rewarded, and thus repeated. Behaviors which are not rewarded will eventually stop. Needless to say, such an approach is most useful in training children and in habit disorders such as smoking or workaholism.

Changing Relationships: *Family therapy*. Family therapists are not interested as much in the internal life of an individual as they are in the relationships in a family. A person with a psychiatric problem, such as depression, will often be seen not as the actual patient, but as the identified patient. Consequently, problem thoughts, feelings, and behaviors are seen in their relationship to family relationships. Solving the problem is usually approached via changing the interactional patterns of family members.

We have discussed four strategies of helping people change as if they are four separate and distinct approaches. This is typically not the case. Rather, most mental health professionals use a combination of strategies, depending on the problem they are trying to solve and their own expertise.

How Psychologists Can Help with Common Problems

In the same way that physical symptoms often signal that we are physically ill, psychological symptoms often signal problems in our psychological world. The seven most common psychological problems include (1) sadness and depression, (2) anxiety problems, (3) panic and phobias, (4) problems recovering emotionally from an accident or crime, (5) addictions, (6) relationship problems, and (7) confusion about life questions or life directions.

For each of these problems in the following pages, we list both the symptoms and the most effective treatment. We suggest that you look through the next section, marking off any symptoms you have. This will help you to know if you might benefit from psychological help, and, if so, what kind of help will likely be best.

Depression and Sadness

While some sadness is a natural part of life, clinical depression is a serious condition which can get in the way of everyday living and requires attention. The following are the major symptoms of depression:

1. Loss of energy (e.g., can't get out of bed in the morning)
2. Loss of interest in life (e.g., nothing is fun anymore)
3. Suicidal feelings
4. Change in appetite and/or body weight
5. Feelings of low self-esteem

You should get an emotional assessment if you have had two or more of these symptoms for more than a couple of weeks. If you ever have the urge to kill yourself or someone else, you should turn to the next chapter for guidance and call a counselor *today*.

What helps? Depression is a very treatable problem. If your doctor diagnoses you with depression, you should be sure to go to a good therapist. Cognitive and behavioral therapeutic strategies are often the most effective in getting rid of these serious symptoms. Psychodynamic, insight-oriented therapy can also help you to understand the causes of your sadness. If you do go to a psychodynamic therapist, be sure to work on applying your insight to everyday life; we have seen more than one person with depression gain plenty of insight from psychodynamic therapy without learning how to apply their insight to become more healthy. If you believe your depression is closely related to things that are going on in your marriage or family, you should pursue marriage or family therapy.

Many people with the more severe forms of depression or those in crisis might benefit from antidepressant medication. Medication is often helpful in treating sleep, appetite, and energy problems. However, when you stop taking medication, these problems will probably come back. Therefore, in planning for the long run, you should always treat depression with psychotherapy, and never just take medication for depression without also getting psychotherapy.

Problems with Anxiety

Like feelings of sadness and depression, occasional feelings of anxiety are also often a part of everyday living. Feelings of anxiety should be expected, for example, while preparing for a major life event, such as marriage, a job interview, or a high school reunion.

However, anxiety can be troublesome when it does not seem linked to a particular cause or if it persists too long. Many people seem to worry all the time and have a hard time controlling this worry. The following signs help to identify this type of anxiety problem:

1. Worry or guilt about several different things
2. Muscles which often feel nervous, restless, achy, shaky
3. Often feel sick to your stomach, have diarrhea, or other digestion problems
4. Trouble falling or staying asleep
5. Have difficulty concentrating, mind goes blank

If two or more of these symptoms get in the way of everyday responsibilities, or if these symptoms are present for more than two months, an emotional assessment is probably needed.

What helps? If you are having problems with anxiety, we recommend that you find a psychotherapist who can use behavioral or cognitive behavioral strategies to reduce the intensity of these worries. A good second choice for dealing with these problems would be a psychodynamic approach, which will help you learn about the meaning of these feelings. Psychodynamic therapists often help you become aware of unconscious feelings or desires which can make you feel anxious. A third choice in treating anxiety is anti-anxiety medication. As with anti-depressant medication, it should only be used after a thorough evaluation and should never take the place of psychotherapy. Finally, anxiety can often be a sign of God moving in your internal world, nudging you in one direction or another. Therefore, if you struggle with anxiety, you may also want to consider working with a spiritual director or pastor as well as a counselor. We will address this further in the next section of the book.

Problems with Panic

While some people have a problem with feelings of anxiety all the time, others have a problem with episodes of panic, often called "panic attacks." The following symptoms typically occur during a panic attack:

1. Rapid heart beat and/or chest pain
2. Difficulty catching your breath
3. Sweating, trembling, shaking
4. Dizziness, lightheadedness, fear of fainting
5. Chills or hot flashes

People who have had a panic attack often fear having another in public, and therefore become afraid of leaving home. These feelings of panic can also happen around specific people, places, or things, causing phobias to develop. People with a phobia begin to panic when they get close to fearful things (e.g., bees, high places, water, etc.), and therefore will often do anything to stay clear of the things they fear.

What Helps? We recommend that you work with a therapist who can use behavioral or cognitive-behavioral techniques. If the problem is severe, we recommend that you ask your therapist about medication.

Problems Recovering Emotionally from an Accident or Crime

Many people who have been through a terrible ordeal or crime often need help to resolve their feelings. Some signs that this has become a problem are:

1. Being unable to get the event out of your mind. For example, you might have dreams or daydreams about it
2. Going to great lengths to avoid anything that makes you think of the hurtful event (e.g., avoiding people who were there or know anything about it)
3. Feeling generally "numb" and unable to experience feelings
4. Feeling generally irritable, distracted, or like you are always "on the lookout"
5. Having a hard time getting to sleep or staying asleep

If your feelings seem to fit into this pattern, you should consider getting an emotional assessment. These feelings often appear after a few days or weeks have gone by where you felt as though you were doing fine.

What helps? If you have suffered some enormous shock or ordeal, you should go to someone who is trained at treating post-traumatic stress disorder, or PTSD. This can be done by counselors with psychodynamic, cognitive, or behavioral backgrounds. Family therapy would not be directly helpful. Medication may be needed initially but will not likely be helpful in the long run.

Addictions

People get addicted to all kinds of things, from alcohol (alcoholism) to their job (workaholism). There are several signs to look for if you feel you may suffer from an addiction.

1. You feel a strong *need* for "it," cannot imagine life without "it," and are restless when not near "it."
2. As time goes on, your need for "it" increases (e.g., whereas working late one night per week used to be enough, now you feel a need to work late three nights).
3. You spend many of your waking hours thinking about "it" and how to get "it."
4. Important commitments to God, yourself, and/or your family are given up because of "it" (e.g., because you are drunk, need to finish a report, or are recovering from overdoing it).

People who are addicted often have a hard time recognizing it themselves. It often takes the caring confrontation of family members, often with the support of friends or a pastor. It is also sometimes helpful for such friends or family to talk with a counselor to learn how to confront someone with an addiction.

What helps? If you or someone you know is addicted to a substance such as alcohol or drugs, medical help is always necessary. Such persons often need a detoxification period, which can become medically dangerous. Persons with addictions should be sure to find a psychotherapist with experience treating addictions. We recommend someone who is familiar with behavioral or cognitive-behavioral strategies, which prevent relapse. This is called "relapse prevention" and is at the heart of treating addictions.

People who have had addictions for a long time often have created other problems for themselves. Consequently, in addition to a recovering addict's individual treatment, marital or family therapy may also be helpful. In addition, family members may benefit from their own psychotherapy to deal with the problems which often arise from living in this situation. These problems are often called "codependent" problems.

There are many self-help groups created for persons who are recovering from addictions, including Alcoholics Anonymous (AA), Codependents Anonymous (CA), Al-Anon, and so on. These groups have been enormously successful, at least in part due to their acknowledgement of the necessity of dependence on God for real, deep healing. We recommend that you use these groups for support as much as possible, with two minor warnings. First, attending these groups is no replacement for a good assessment. You should always start with a well-trained psychotherapist to clarify what issues you need to address. Second, these groups are only as healthy as the people who attend any given meeting. Therefore, feel free to "shop around" until you find a group that feels "right," and always feel free to leave a meeting if you get the sense that it might be harmful to you.

Relationship Problems

God has created us to be in life-giving relationships with one another. Yet many people find it nearly impossible to find meaningful relationships with compatible people. Signs of relationship problems include the following:

1. A series of unfulfilling relationships which seem to repeat themselves (e.g., a woman divorces an alcoholic and abusive man, only to remarry a second man with the same tendencies)

2. Difficulty making or keeping satisfying friendships or intimate relationships
3. Feeling like certain groups of people are not trustworthy, such as authority figures, men, women, or some racial group
4. A problem in a close relationship that has stayed the same or worsened despite having worked on it for more than six months

If any of these symptoms apply to you, you will probably benefit from a personality assessment. Like addictions, relationship problems can sometimes be difficult for a person to identify about him- or herself. Therefore, people often need a friend, family member, or minister to lovingly point out the problem they seem to be having.

What helps? If you are currently in a marital relationship which you are unable to heal on your own, marital or family therapy is probably the best choice for you to pursue. The bonus here is that you will learn from your spouse or partner how you make him or her feel. This can be a wonderful learning experience. You may also want to attend a marital enrichment program. These programs have been shown to be very helpful at resolving conflict and increasing the vitality of relationships.

If you are not in a relationship, you would probably do well to pursue more psychodynamic, insight-oriented psychotherapy. While this kind of help generally takes longer (often six months or more of weekly sessions), this amount of time is often necessary for deeper and more meaningful insights to emerge.

Confusion about Life Questions or Life Direction

Living in today's world is often disorienting and confusing; it is not uncommon for people to feel lost or confused now and then. However, many people get stuck in their confusion and remain confused for several months, and in some cases, even years. These are signs of this problem:

1. This confusion persists more than four months.

2. Efforts to talk it through with family and friends have not proven helpful.
3. Efforts to pray it through have either seemed very difficult or have not seemed to help.
4. You fear having made an enormously wrong decision (e.g., getting married, choosing a career).
5. Life no longer seems enjoyable or meaningful; what was once invigorating is now a chore.

If you have experienced two or more of these symptoms, you may want to consider getting a personality or emotional assessment.

What helps? If you face this sort of confusion you will probably benefit most from a therapist who will help to cultivate insight and clarify your values and spiritual commitments. Therefore, our first recommendation would be to go to a psychodynamic therapist or a spiritual director. For this type of problem, be sure you find a professional who shares your value commitments. We will address this issue in depth in the next two chapters.

The Benefits of Psychotherapy

What can we expect to change when we submit ourselves to the healing work of good psychotherapy? Can we expect a total relief of all psychological discomfort? Can we expect to become "self-actualized"? Can we expect an end to our lifelong struggles? Psychologists and other mental health professionals have been studying the effects of psychotherapy for many years and have reached some important conclusions about the benefits of psychotherapy.

1. Psychotherapy helps to remove painful symptoms.

The first benefit often gained from psychotherapy is simply the removal of unwanted symptoms. There are several examples which illustrate this positive effect. People who have ongoing anxious thoughts that will not go away can often find relief through psychotherapy. Similarly, those who struggle with sinful behavior, such as workaholism, can often change their behavior. Finally, those who struggle with difficult feelings, such as lust, often grow in insight, which helps to understand and reduce the intensity of such feelings.

2. Psychotherapy helps people see life more truthfully.

Second, psychotherapy helps people to see life more truthfully. However, truth often causes pain, and our unconscious minds are determined to avoid pain whenever possible! We then slip back into old patterns of behavior as we attempt to cope with a reality that is too difficult to bear.

For example, I (Dr. Hart) once worked with a group of women who had been severely sexually abused. Each told a story of a series of painful and broken relationships, all of which were marked by confusion and promiscuous, sinful behavior. These women found relief from their promiscuity only when they faced the deep betrayal, pain, and shame they experienced as young children when they were first sexually violated. The truth they had to face was painful. But once they dealt with their underlying pain, their symptoms diminished.

3. Psychotherapy helps people live life with more freedom, control, and spontaneity.

The third way psychotherapy can be beneficial is to help increase one's ability to live life with more freedom, control, and spontaneity. Some psychologists call this change "increased ego strength."

Consider the life of a cockroach. When a light is turned on, a cockroach runs the other way. It always works that way. Cockroaches have an innate fear of light. Even if they are eating good food off your counter, they will still run when you turn the light on. There is no pause between the stimulus (the light coming on) and the response (running). We would say, therefore, that a cockroach has no choice but to run.

Humans, of course, are different. For us, there is a pause between stimulus and response. Within that pause we experience freedom. We are free to react. We are free to pray. We are free to love, and we are free to sin. We are free to imagine a totally different response. Therapy helps increase the pause between stimulus and response, so that people are more free to choose their actions.

Consider the typical workaholic. He works fourteen-hour days, six days per week. Try asking him why he works so much. He will undoubtedly tell you "because I have no choice." Observe him as he sits in his office and his boss comes to him with yet another project and asks, "Can you do this project too?" The workaholic experiences no choice. He hears his boss say, "Do this project too."

As people slowly learn how their life experiences have contributed to a sinful way of life, they gradually see through this web of pressure and influence and begin to experience some freedom to choose differently.

But Isn't Jesus Enough?

Just a week ago I (Dr. Hart) was on a radio program back East. The host was a friend I have known for many years, a Lutheran pastor with great insight into the human condition. The first caller was a woman named Linda. She got right to the point: "Why must we be concerned about this psychology stuff? Isn't Jesus enough?"

I understood exactly what she was trying to say. She was asking: If God has provided for all our healing, then why do we need human intervention. Can't Jesus do it all?

I could give only one response. "Yes, Jesus is enough!" No doubt about it. But then I explained that the question doesn't go far enough. For instance, if I discover that I have cancer, isn't Jesus enough? Of course he is! With Jesus I can bear any pain, any hardship, any catastrophe. He can give me the courage to be brave and face death if I must. If he chooses he can also heal my cancer.

But here comes the rub: does this mean I don't seek medical help? If the doctor tells me that I can be cured of my cancer with an operation, do I turn around and say, "Sorry, doctor, but Jesus is enough for me; I don't need your help"? I can, but it wouldn't be very smart, and I doubt if it would please God either. Yet this is what many emotionally troubled Christians do with their problems. Just because they cannot see the cause of their problem doesn't mean that the problem isn't real and cannot be helped.

Yes, God *can* heal us. But he doesn't always, and it isn't always miraculous. Sometimes it is through the hands of a surgeon or an internist, and sometimes it is through the help of a good counselor or psychologist. They too can be what John Wesley called "means of God's grace."

It is of course crucial that you find a qualified and helpful therapist. In the next chapter, we will show you where to look for a therapist and how to make sure he or she is qualified to help you.

Chapter 5

Choosing a Good Psychotherapist

The task of finding a therapist poses a unique problem: the need for counseling often arises when you are least able to make good decisions, such as during a crisis or time of confusion. Just when you need to make a clear-headed decision, you need someone to help you! It's as if you were severely farsighted and had lost your glasses in a darkened room. You need your glasses to find your glasses! In the same way, in times of psychological stress, you often need help to find help.

In this chapter, we have tried to act as your "glasses," taking some of the guesswork out of the procedure of finding a therapist so that you can quickly and effectively find the help you need.

Choosing the Right Setting for Therapy

When you begin your quest to find a psychotherapist, you will likely be surprised at the number of options you have at your disposal. Psychotherapists work in many diverse settings, including community mental health clinics, university counseling centers, hospitals, churches, and private offices. Each setting will come with some advantages and disadvantages.

In general, the setting of therapy falls into one of two categories: public clinics or private offices.

Public Clinics

Public clinics, such as community mental health centers, university counseling centers, and social service agencies, typically receive supplemental funding from university training programs, governmental programs, or church organizations and operate on a "sliding fee" basis. Such subsidized funding typically allows public clinics to provide psychotherapy at a reduced fee, often based on income. This lower fee is the primary advantage to seeking therapy in a public clinic.

But there is a second advantage to going to a public clinic, especially one linked to a university or graduate school counseling center: The psychotherapists in training often interact with many other professionals and have more varied supervision available to them.

There are disadvantages to public agencies, however, especially if you are concerned for your spiritual growth. First, because demand for low-fee psychotherapy is often greater than the ability to meet the demand, the number of sessions you receive may be limited. Consequently, you may be on a waiting list for several weeks or months before you get seen, then have the number of total sessions available to you sharply limited.

Second, clinics often ask you to go through an intake procedure, then assign you to a given therapist based on your need, not your preference. This decreases your freedom to find a therapist with whom you feel comfortable.

Third, unless the clinic is expressly Christian, your therapist is not likely to resonate with your faith.

Private Offices

Private offices rely on fees paid by clients and/or insurance companies. This setting also has its tradeoffs. On the positive side, you can choose a therapist whom you like and see that therapist for as long as you want or can afford. Similarly, you can often avoid an intake process conducted by a third person and meet directly with the therapist you prefer.

On the down side, you will typically pay more to see someone in private practice. With the clamp-down on insurance reimbursements by managed care companies, there will also be a restriction on the number of sessions that your health insurance will cover.

It is worth noting that while psychotherapy offered in public clinics is often assumed to be of lower quality than that offered in private clinics, this is not universally true. In fact, you will find both helpful and unhelpful psychotherapists in all types of settings. This is why you need to consider other important characteristics of a potential therapist before entering a therapy relationship.

Professional Training

Throughout this book we have referred to "psychotherapists" generically. However, many professions offer psychotherapy, so when it comes to identifying persons competent to do psychotherapy, the term is not helpful at all! Furthermore, the titles "counselor," "therapist," and "hypnotist" are not regulated in many states. Almost anyone can hang up a shingle with one of these titles.

Furthermore, because different professional groups have different standards of practice, the training of those who may legitimately call themselves psychotherapists can vary from one to ten years. It is crucial, therefore, that you be aware of the kind and level of training a psychotherapist has received.

In addition to finding out what kind of training a psychotherapist has received, you need to know where a psychotherapist received this training. Most complete their training at accredited universities and professional schools. This means that the professional community has recognized the program as meeting appropriate quality standards. Programs that have lost or have never received accreditation should be treated with caution. Some may provide good training, but others are mere diploma mills. Find out all you can about the accreditation of the program your chosen therapist has graduated from. A list of accrediting agencies, with addresses, is provided in Appendix A.

What follows is a description of the training and expertise of various mental health professionals.

Clinical Psychologist (Ph.D., Psy.D.)

Clinical psychologists attend four years of college plus four or more years of graduate school, plus one or more years of full-time supervised training. Some (but not most) states allow master's level psychologists (M.A.) to practice independently. This requires one to two years of graduate study plus supervised experience.

Expertise: Clinical psychologists are usually very good at helping people clarify what their problems and strengths are (assessment) and helping people solve problems and heal mentally and emotionally (psychotherapy).

Caution: Be sure to clarify that a person is a *clinical* or *counseling* psychologist; other areas of specialization in psychology, such as industrial, experimental, or educational psychology do not emphasize psychotherapy or treat severe disturbances or abnormal behavior.

Psychiatry (M.D., D.O.)

Psychiatrists first receive training in medicine. This requires four years of college plus four years of medical school. While not required by law, most psychiatrists also complete a three-year residency program working in a psychiatric facility.

Expertise: Psychiatrists are trained to find the right medications to help with psychological problems. Many psychiatrists also do psychotherapy.

Caution: Foundational training in medicine can sometimes lead to an overdependence on techniques such as medication and electroconvulsive therapy. Sessions may also be less than thirty minutes, which really does not constitute psychotherapy.

Social Work (M.S.W.)

This degree requires four years of college plus one to two years of graduate training and supervised experience.

Expertise: While primary training focuses on community resources, some social workers specialize in psychiatric or clinical work which includes additional training in psychotherapy.

Caution: Social workers do not typically have advanced cognitive and emotional assessment skills, and many do not choose to receive training as psychotherapists.

Marriage and Family Counselors or Therapists (M.F.C.C., M.A.)

This degree requires four years of college plus two to four years of graduate training and supervised experience.

Expertise: Marriage and family therapists are usually good at helping troubled relationships to heal.

Caution: Despite primary training in therapy with couples and families, many MFCC's without appropriate training offer assessment and psychotherapy to severely disturbed individuals.

Mental Health Counselor

This title is used by persons with four years of college plus two to four years of graduate study (M.A., M.Ed., Ed.D., or Ph.D.) in a mental-health-related field. Unfortunately, states vary widely in their regulation of this title.

Expertise: Certified mental health counselors typically are trained to help with areas such as career, vocational, rehabilitation, or general mental health counseling, depending on their training.

Caution: Clarify licensure status and nature of training.

Psychiatric Nurse (R.N., B.S.N., or M.S.N.)

These degrees require a minimum of four years of college and often have two or more years of graduate training.

Expertise: Psychiatric nurses typically work with psychiatric hospitals, and often have an area of specialty for individual counseling.

Caution: This title is not closely monitored in many states. Specific nature of training should be clarified.

Licensure

In addition to the training psychotherapists receive, they also should be licensed or certified to provide psychotherapy. In the United States, licensure is regulated by each state. Before a person can receive a license from the state, three criteria must usually be met. First, the person must complete an acceptable educational program. Second, a person must prove that he or she has had a certain amount of supervised experience. Third, a person must usually pass a written examination and sometimes a second oral interview.

Licensure or certification means that the state has put its stamp of approval on the professional. It tells you that a person probably knows a great deal about psychotherapy. However, it does not tell you everything you need to know. While a person may be able to pass graduate school classes and pass a state's multiple choice examination, certification does not tell you if the person is a gifted therapist. You still have to check out a therapist's character and spirituality to see if it fits with yours.

Professional and Organizational Memberships

Therapists not only are licensed but also join professional organizations and sometimes become certified by these organizations after having completed certain requirements. This ensures two things: the therapist continues to update his or her therapy skills, and the therapist holds himself or herself accountable to a body of practitioners. Both are important!

Membership in a professional organization usually tells you that the therapist has an interest in a particular area and that he or she has contact with the larger professional community. To become a member of an organization, a therapist must usually go through an application process, pay dues, and sometimes get another therapist to co-sign the application.

Some professional groups, such as the American Psychological Association (APA), require their members to adhere to very strict ethical principles, principles designed to protect the consumer. Psychologists who violate these principles run the risk of having their membership revoked. All in all, we believe you should be suspicious of a therapist who is not a participating member of the organization representing his or her profession. However, keep in mind that simple membership does not guarantee that a therapist is competent within his or her area of specialty.

Some professionals also become certified by specialist professional groups. This usually means that a person has passed an examination and has been judged by other experts in the field as being competent in that specialty.

For example, after practicing for more than four years, psychologists can receive board certification in psychotherapy or other specialties. Such psychologists then have the abbreviation "ABPP" after their degree. Similarly, psychiatrists can become board certified after completing a three-year residency, and social workers can become certified after two years of clinical practice (ACSW). It takes hard work to receive this type of certification, and it should be understood as a significant vote of confidence in the professional. However, as with the other criteria we've discussed, it is no guarantee of a good fit with you. For further information on professional organizations and board certifications, contact the groups listed in Appendix A.

Taken together, we see professional memberships and board certifications to be the signs of a potentially good therapist who will be able to help you. In addition, therapists whose work is deemed unethical or incompetent run the risk of losing their memberships and board certifications in such groups and/or being required to undergo additional training or treatment themselves. This gives them more to lose if they do not treat you adequately.

Orientation and Specialty Area

People are complex, and human problems are unique. No two people have ever had the exact same experience and problem. However, despite the absolute uniqueness of every human being, many human problems are similar. One reason psychotherapy has been found to be effective is because therapists, after seeing the same kind of problem many times, learn what information, techniques, and skills are most helpful.

Find out what kinds of people and what kinds of problems your prospective therapist has been trained to help. Many psychologists call themselves "generalists" and claim they can work with almost any problem. They are the equivalent of the internist in medicine.

However, psychotherapists should be able to tell you (1) their area of primary expertise and (2) areas for which they have not been trained. As in medicine, everyone is not trained to do everything!

Professionals who cannot give satisfactory answers to these two questions do not know the limits of their competence. We believe you should stay away from such professionals.

Values and Psychotherapy

For many years, therapists were trained to do "value-free" psychotherapy. In other words, people believed that a therapist could help a person without imposing his or her values on a client. We no longer believe this today. All therapy is loaded with the value system of the therapist. In fact, research in this area has clearly shown that people who undergo psychotherapy often change their values. This means that people often change their minds about what they think is most important, morally correct, and virtuous. This may sound scary, and it should. We have found that many therapists, while agreeing to work with Christians, do not share a love for God or a desire to live a life consistent with the gospel. Such therapists can indirectly and unintentionally lead people away from their Christian life.

Therefore, you should examine the spiritual and religious background of all potential therapists. Many professionals would disagree with this and say a good atheist therapist is better than a bad Christian therapist. If these are your only choices, we might recommend no therapy at all. If a therapist cannot fully cooperate with your goal of living near to God, he or she is probably not worth your investment of time and money.

Personal Qualifications of the Therapist

Once you know a prospective therapist's professional background, credentials, and value commitments, you should have a good idea about how competent a therapist generally is. You then must consider whether a therapist is good for you.

As we have already mentioned, while good credentials are crucial, when it is time to get down to work, psychotherapy is all about sitting in a room and talking with another human being. And regardless of how perfectly suited a therapist is for you on paper, if you do not like the person or if you feel uncomfortable with him or her, therapy is probably not going to be productive. Consequently, you should look at three subjective aspects of your prospective therapist in order to determine compatibility.

First, consider the personal aspects of your therapist. In general, the age and cultural background of a therapist, number of years he or she has practiced, and the quality of his or her nonprofessional life are helpful indicators of whether you will be comfortable with him or her. If a therapist's nonprofessional life is in shambles, you would be well advised to look elsewhere for help.

Second, consider a prospective therapist's interpersonal style and basic personality. Personality clashes can occur between therapist and client as easily as they can occur on the job or with neighbors. While some are extroverts, others are introverts. While some are passive, others are more active; while some are warm and demonstrative, others are cold and reserved. Chances are you will be most comfortable with a certain mixture of these characteristics. It is up to you to find a therapist with whom you feel most comfortable.

One word of caution, however, on matching your personality to your therapist's. If you are an extrovert, you may at first be drawn to another extrovert. Similarly, if you are an introvert you may prefer a like-minded therapist. But this may not be best for you if your style is part of your problem. An introvert who is socially withdrawn may learn more from a gregarious, outgoing therapist than a detached, reclusive, or shy therapist. Similarly, if you talk too much, a reflective, thoughtful therapist may have a lot to teach you. So you need not only to consider your comfort level but also your social needs when selecting a therapist who is a good fit for you.

Third, you should find a therapist who seems to genuinely care about you and your situation. This is often a sign that he or she has the healing gifts necessary to do good therapy. Many therapists come across as distant "technicians" and "experts." Don't let that intimidate you. Instead, you should look for a therapist that you can connect with and feel good about.

Chapter 6

How to Get Good Therapy

If you have gone through a painful and soul-searching process and concluded that you need or desire psychotherapy for healing, you may not know where to begin to prepare yourself for the experience. What traps should you avoid? How can you maximize your therapy? The following steps will help you prepare for a successful outcome.

Rule Out Physical Causes

Many symptoms of psychological distress, such as anxiety, sadness, lack of energy, confusion, and memory problems can be the result of physical problems. Therefore, we recommend that you start with your family physician to ensure that you are in good health. Physicians are sometimes able to determine if a biological problem is causing psychological symptoms.

Establish Goals for Therapy

Before you select a therapist, be clear about what help you want. Clarify exactly what needs to change and set some goals. Ask yourself some basic questions: What would I like to be different in my life? What is hard for me to do? What feelings seem to get in my way? How are the relationships in my life working out? What kind of feedback do people give me about myself?

If it is difficult for you to put your finger on exactly what it is you want from therapy, you might want to first talk to your pastor or trusted confidant about your confusion and try to increase your understanding of how God is leading you to change and grow.

Be honest with yourself from the start. If you know that you are not willing to experience pain and confusion as part of the healing process, it is probably the wrong time to start therapy.

Create a List of Potential Psychotherapists

Where do you go to find names? There are several reliable resources. First, friends who have been in therapy are often the best source of names. It is often particularly beneficial to ask someone who has seen more than one therapist, or someone who has appeared to benefit from therapy.

Second, pastors can often be helpful sources of information. Remember, pastors make many referrals all the time and often continue to see parishioners after they have started in therapy. This places them in a good position to be familiar with the effectiveness of a therapist's work.

Third, psychotherapists can often make referrals to competent colleagues. You may consider this if you know of a therapist with an excellent reputation but are not able to see her because her caseload is full, you have already developed a non-professional friendship, or the fee is unaffordable.

Fourth, physicians are also a source of referrals. However, physicians sometimes favor medical explanations for problems and often will refer you to another physician (psychiatrist), even though your problem may be best treated by a non-medical professional.

Directories in your local library are an alternative to personal referrals. Psychiatrists are listed in the *American Psychiatric Association Directory* or in the *Directory of Medical Specialists* if they have received board certification; psychologists are listed in the *American Psychological Association Directory* and the *National Register for Health Service Providers in Psychology*; social workers can be found in the membership directory of the *National Association of Social*

Workers or in its *Register of Clinical Social Workers.* The *Yellow Pages* are a frequently used source of names, but the advertisers listed there may or may not be licensed.

Finally, many referral services can be found in telephone books and classified advertisement sections of the newspaper. Such services offer to put you in touch with the most appropriate professionals. While many of these services are indeed helpful, these can also be a marketing gimmick for groups of therapists who are simply trying to increase their own business.

Call and Screen Therapists

We cannot stress this step strongly enough. An initial telephone call may save you a lot of trouble later.

Call your list of potential therapists on the phone. When you make the call, you will probably not be able to speak with the therapist right away. Either the therapist or the intake worker will call you back. You may be asked to complete an intake form, either over the phone or in person, before you can interview a therapist. Before you go through this process to determine if he or she is interested in seeing you, you should ask several of the following questions:

- What is the fee range, and how is the fee determined?
- What hours is the clinic or therapist available?
- How much input toward the choice of therapist will I have if there is more than one therapist in the practice?
- What kind of training has he or she had?
- What kind of supervision will he or she receive if the person is still in training?
- How long has he or she been practicing?
- What kind of license does he or she have?
- What is his or her orientation and specialty area?
- Is there a brochure describing the clinic or private practice? If so, ask to have one sent to you.
- What is the charge, if any, for the first session (often called an "initial consultation")?

Many people believe that therapists should not charge for the first session. However, therapists, like lawyers and physicians, sell their time. Therefore, if a therapist is going to take time to help you find good therapy, he or she may have to charge for it.

We recommend that you ask as many of the above questions as possible and seek satisfactory answers before you ever walk into the therapist's office. Once you have these answers, you should be able to narrow your list of prospective therapists to two or three. You are then ready to schedule a first interview with each.

Interview Prospective Therapists

Therapy is such a personal experience that you should always ask for an initial interview, and then go home and think about it before you commit yourself to therapy. The first session is a critical one for both you and the therapist to find out if the two of you can work well together. Most therapists will want to find out what brings you to therapy. Otherwise, they will not be able to make an informed decision about whether or not they would be comfortable with or capable of being your therapist.

Some therapists (particularly the good ones) will decline to become your therapist if they discover that they have little experience working with your issues or have a significant conflict in values. Because of this, you need to have thought about your problems and the expectations you have for therapy, so you can talk about them during this first session.

While it is important for the therapist to hear about you during this first session, it is also important that you interview the therapist. Remember, your primary goal during this session should not be to start solving your problem, but to determine if the therapist is likely to be helpful. You should be the one who structures the first session.

Regardless of what you say on the telephone, many therapists will assume that you have come to their office to begin therapy. If the therapist takes charge of the session and pursues details or seems to be following a structured interview, do not be intimidated; you are the one paying for the services, so you get to call the shots. Interrupt if you have to, and be sure to get answers to your questions. Remember, you can ask a therapist any question you want to. Be sure to ask questions in the following areas: training and licensure, areas of expertise, value commitments, personal integrity, interpersonal style, and fees. However, ethically speaking, the only questions therapists are obliged to answer are those involving their professional training, licensure, and expertise.

Training and Licensure

Clarify any questions about training and licensure that were not answered over the telephone. Look for training in a recognizable program, some type of license, and membership in one or more professional organizations.

Areas of Expertise

Clarify areas of expertise and non-expertise. Ask: What kinds of problems do you usually work with? What area do you consider your strongest? What age group? Are there areas or problems for which you would refer me to someone else, like a pastor, psychiatrist, or marriage counselor? Look for acknowledgment of limitations and specialties and willingness to refer or work with other professionals.

Value Commitments

Attempt to elicit therapists' value commitments. Ask: What does it mean to you for a person to be healthy? What does successful therapy look like to you? If we were to discover that my spouse does not meet my needs, would you suggest or consider divorce for me? Are you committed to a life of faith or the kingdom of God? Do not look for absolute answers and total agreement on all matters, only on those that are most important to you. Instead, discern whether the overall world view of this person seems godly and attractive. Also, therapists commonly talk around questions without answering them. This might simply indicate a desire to understand your concern. In any case, be sure to pursue the question until you are satisfied with the answer.

Personal Integrity

Ask: Do you receive supervision or have you had personal psychotherapy yourself? If you and I were to get stuck, would you go to another professional for help? Look for an openness to talk about these issues and a lack of defensiveness. Ask yourself if this person is hiding behind his or her role more than you are comfortable with. Honesty and openness are essential characteristics for a good therapist.

Interpersonal Style

You will not feel comfortable with every therapist, just as you won't feel comfortable with every lawyer or physician you meet. There needs to be a "fit" between you, and this fit will depend largely on the therapist's ability to make you feel comfortable by exhibiting good interpersonal skills. Remember, it is not your responsibility to impress or make the therapist comfortable; it is the therapist's responsibility to make you comfortable. Ask yourself the following questions after you leave the therapist's office: Did you feel respected? Did you feel accepted? Did the therapist seem comfortable with you or was he or she threatened? Did you feel comfortable or threatened?

Fees

Clarify and confirm questions about fees for therapy. Ask: What is your fee? Would you see me for less than that? How does your billing system work? Do you have a policy for late payments? Will I be charged for sessions I miss? Does my health insurance cover part of my therapy? Are you a provider in my health plan? Can you refer me to someone else whose fee I can afford or who is covered? Look for an ability to address the issue of payment of fees openly and nondefensively. Be prepared in advance to say how much you can genuinely afford. Money issues can be a big problem initially. Some therapists are not open to negotiating fees, so don't be offended if they refuse your suggestions. Remember, for many therapists, their only source of income is their fees.

If going in to a therapist's office and asking all these questions sounds too intimidating, we suggest you consider bringing someone else with you to this first interview. Ask a trustworthy friend or confidant, and discuss what you are looking for before you go in. Call the therapist beforehand and warn him or her that you will have someone with you. Afterward, remember that the therapy is for you, and use your friend's advice only as it helps you to make your decision. Some therapists will not allow you to bring a friend with you. We recommend that you simply avoid any therapist who is intimidated by this request.

Pray

Once you have gone through each of these steps, take time to pray over your decision. You do not need to rush into therapy. Be persistent and patient until you find a therapist who feels right for you. Look for a feeling of confidence that you can trust the therapist with your deepest secrets. Trust is the key to good therapy. Without it you will not open up honestly enough.

One word of caution is appropriate at this point. Don't expect a strong feeling of confidence in your chosen therapist at first. This grows with time. If it doesn't, then it is a sure sign that the two of you don't match. However, unconditional trust sometimes takes a little time to develop.

In the next chapter we will explore ways in which you can get the most out of your therapy.

Chapter 7

Getting the Most Out of Psychotherapy

Therapy is expensive. There's no doubt about that. But before we look at the ways you can reduce your fees, let's first look at the question of fees.

Often, people will not seek help because they think they do not deserve it or they fear they cannot afford it. However, if those same people were to face a life-threatening illness, such as cancer, they would be quick to find help. Why, then, should they neglect their emotional health—particularly if their emotional illness interferes with their ability to be a loving spouse, good parent, and productive worker? Money should never stand in the way of getting the help needed.

In addition, money can positively affect therapy. Paying a fee indicates a commitment to growth and healing. Many clinicians have observed that clients who pay for therapy, no matter how little, tend to take it more seriously and work harder.

Pursuing therapy does entail a major commitment of resources. Sessions with a well-seasoned therapist often cost over $90 an hour. In some cities, $150 per session is not uncommon. With this kind of expense in mind, most people jump to the conclusion that they simply cannot afford psychotherapy.

But the news is not all bad. There are ways to get the psychotherapy you need at a reasonable cost. By following several hints, you can be sure to get the most for your money without breaking the bank. Here are our suggestions.

Explore Your Health Insurance Options

Call your health insurance company or health maintenance organization (HMO) and find out if mental health services are covered. If they are, clarify what types of service are covered. If your health insurance does not include mental health coverage, see if there is an Employee Assistance Plan (EAP) at your place of employment.

EAPs are specifically designed to offer counseling to employees and their families for a low cost. You may be covered by an EAP and not know it, so it is worth calling your personnel office.

Finally, if you discover that you do not have mental health benefits, find out if your spouse or another family member who has mental health benefits can add you to the policy. It is often cost effective to pay a monthly premium in exchange for being covered for mental health benefits.

Explore Options for Lower Fees

There are several options for finding lower-cost therapy. First, as we suggested in the previous chapter, many public clinics offer therapy on a sliding scale based on your income. Therefore, if your income is low or if you are unemployed, you might want to focus your efforts on public clinics. Most cities have publically funded Mental Health clinics that provide services at little or no cost. Of course, these services are usually available for only more serious problems, but it is possible that some readers are troubled enough to qualify for help through one of these agencies.

Second, many therapists in private practice will lower their rates if you genuinely can't afford them and the therapist is not over-committed. But you have to ask.

Therapists are often willing to reduce their fees for several reasons. First, many therapists will offer a reduced rate if you and your issues are of interest to them. This may sound a little strange to a lay person, but sometimes a therapist develops an interest in a particular type of problem and wants to see as many patients with this problem as possible for professional interest reasons. The therapist may be doing some research or writing a book on the topic. You can benefit from this focused interest. Also, some may be seeking further or specialized certification and may need to see particular patients to complete their assignments.

Others will offer a lower rate to persons with financial hardship out of a sense of obligation to their profession. Every profession encourages "pro bono" services, and psychology and counseling are no exceptions.

Yet others will offer a lower rate if you have been referred by a particular person or referral source they value. When, say, a pastor often refers parishioners to a particular therapist, that therapist may give special consideration to a pastor who makes a plea for a low fee. Those who can pay make it possible for the therapist to offer services to those who can't by subsidizing the total cost of the service.

Many clients are reluctant to ask for a fee adjustment out of fear that they might be insulting the therapist. Let me be frank on this point. Any therapist who feels insulted because you ask for some consideration on fees is probably not worth seeing. Most therapists are not offended by such requests. They see your request as a willingness to be vulnerable, to put your ego on the line and risk being rejected. A healthy therapist will accept your request as perfectly natural, even if it cannot be accommodated.

The bottom line is this: Never assume you cannot ask a therapist for a reduced fee. You certainly can. If you are honest with the therapist about what you can afford and what he or she is able to accept, then there need not be any hard feelings about the final outcome. Just don't be offended yourself if your request isn't granted.

If you do negotiate a lower fee due to your own financial hardship, it is extremely important that you also clarify with your therapist how the fee will change when your financial conditions change. Otherwise, you might find yourself hiding issues from your therapist that are related to your finances. This will negatively impact your therapy and can cause significant harm to your therapy relationship.

A third way to cut the cost of psychotherapy is to contact a graduate school of psychology or a training institute for therapists in your area. Training programs often offer four- to eight-month treatment programs at a markedly reduced rate. This provides training experience for their therapists and very affordable therapy for you.

Before pursuing this option, consider these points. First and foremost, you must determine how much and what kind of supervision the therapist-in-training will be getting. For example, many trainees receive supervision from well-seasoned therapists. Others only receive infrequent and mediocre supervision. The effectiveness of your therapy will depend very much on the quality of supervision given, so be sure to ask detailed questions before you agree to this kind of therapy.

A fourth way to save money is to seek an alternative form of therapy. Some therapists, for example, might suggest that you pursue group therapy. Group therapy often costs about half that of individual therapy. Group psychotherapy is usually helpful for those who wish to develop better interpersonal skills and learn how to express their feelings more clearly. However, group therapy is not suitable for everyone and does not always allow you to delve deeply into your own issues. Others get to talk about their problems also.

Some therapists might suggest that you take medication (called "pharmacotherapy") or undergo electroconvulsive therapy (ECT) if you are severely depressed. These therapies are often very necessary for serious psychological difficulties. However, make sure you have come to trust your therapist before embarking on this course, as it presents a much bigger risk to your mental, emotional, and physical health, if mismanaged, than does psychotherapy. If such interventions are suggested, get a second opinion before you submit to these treatments.

Finally, the representative of your HMO or EAP may suggest that you go to a seminar or workshop designed to teach you supplementary skills to undergird your therapy. Addiction support groups or stress management seminars would be good examples. They typically cost you very little, if anything, so we recommend that you take advantage of them when possible, but do not think of these as substitutes for therapy.

Keep Your Therapy Structured and Focused

Psychotherapy is often expensive because if it is not focused, it ends up being endless. Unfortunately, many therapy relationships have very little structure, so they go on week after week, waiting for difficulties to arise and solving them as they come up. This fosters a dependency where clients believe they cannot leave therapy until they have no more problems left to solve. Rather than mastering the skills needed to deal generally with their problems, clients focus on their present problem in too much detail.

Dependency also occurs when clients take a childish approach to therapy, waiting for the therapist to call the shots and determine when to terminate. Unfortunately, the longer you stay in therapy, the more money you pay. Therefore, even good therapists are often reluctant to help you resolve your dilemma in the shortest amount of time or suggest you end therapy when your goals have been met. They leave it up to you—so take control!

So, to prevent your therapy from transforming into the "endless" variety, come to therapy prepared. Before you walk into the therapist's office, clarify for yourself what it is you want from therapy, and what you want to be different. If you can't figure it out for yourself, make this the first goal of therapy!

While the first few sessions typically move very slowly as you and your therapist get to know each other, we suggest you work with your therapist to define your goals for therapy by the fourth or fifth session. Then monitor these goals every month to be sure you stay on track.

By monitoring your work you can stay focused and know when you have met your goals for therapy. This helps you know when your problem is resolved and the time has come to either end therapy or set a new goal. By taking this approach, you will find yourself solving one issue or problem at a time. This keeps your energy focused and increases the likelihood that you will accomplish your goals. Remember, you can always go back to therapy at a later date as other issues arise in your life, often with the same therapist.

We should mention that there are some situations where long-term therapy (e.g., weekly therapy for more than six months and even lasting several years) is helpful. For example, often mental health providers themselves engage in ongoing therapy for long periods due to the difficult nature of their work. They need to resolve their own problems outside of their client's therapy and not allow personal problems to get in the way. Similarly, individuals with chronic mental illnesses or history of severe emotional trauma find ongoing long-term therapy beneficial, if not essential.

However, for most emotional or situational problems that are not severe, short-term therapy (less than twenty sessions) to mid-term therapy (less than forty-five sessions) is all that is needed. Research shows that knowing there is a definite limit to the therapy helps to bring about an improvement within the stipulated period. Also, follow-up therapy of just one or two sessions at a time over several years helps to entrench the original therapy and prevent relapses.

Make the Most of Each Individual Session

Your time with your therapist can often be emotionally draining and intellectually challenging. There is a limit, therefore, to what you can accomplish in one session. However, our experience has been that clients often waste time by not being forthright or honest. They leave critical bits of information to the end, or resist opening up.

Therefore, if you are going to make the most of the session itself, commit yourself to total self-disclosure and to reflection about the therapy both before and after your sessions. This will help you stay focused within the session itself.

Furthermore, don't waste time. For example, we have seen many clients who persist in coming to therapy five or ten minutes late and out of breath. They were trying to run several errands before coming! In such situations it typically takes at least another five to ten minutes before they are settled down and ready to do the work of therapy.

Similarly, many people try to see their psychotherapist on their lunch hour. While this may feel like an efficient use of time, you might find yourself unable to go into deeper emotional issues, knowing that you may not be able to "pull it together" in the ten minutes you have between the end of your session and when you need to be back at work. Instead, when possible, give yourself time both before and after therapy to pray, write in a diary or journal, or go for a relaxing walk. This will maximize your therapy and help you stay focused while with your therapist.

One more point on the matter of saving time. If your therapist is often late, kick up a fuss! Sure, we all have to work around genuine emergencies, but being late may be a bad habit that needs correction—even in psychotherapists!

Use "Adjunctive Resources" as Much as Possible

Once you have made the commitment to change your life through therapy, you can do many things to enhance and supplement your therapy experience.

Therapy often leads clients to be more reflective about childhood. It may be helpful if you try to remember how you learned to understand the world during your childhood. Because these memories are often difficult to recover, you might find it helpful to pull out photo albums, old pictures, letters and the like, and write about your memories in a diary or journal. This will give you raw material on which to work in therapy.

A second adjunct resource is the use of books, often referred to as "bibliotherapy." Many effective self-help books can help you learn about problems you are having. However, we strongly recommend that you discuss what books you want to read with your therapist before you start reading them. Many self-help books, while seemingly appropriate, cause clients to become more confused or troubled. It's not unlike reading a medical textbook when you have an undefined illness. If you're not careful, you end up believing you've got every problem in the book!

Pray Throughout Your Therapy

If you have ever had surgery, you will have learned an important lesson about the healing process: While surgeons can cut, open, remove, replace, and stitch, only God and your body can finally heal the wound.

If the surgery is to be successful, you have to keep your wound clean, eat nutritious food to increase tissue building, take antibiotics to keep out infection, and get plenty of rest. Without these the surgery is useless.

The same is true for psychological wounds. While a therapist can often help open psychological wounds, reveal the cause of emotional pain, and suggest new ways of thinking, only God can bring the miracle of emotional healing. We strongly suggest, therefore, that you make a prayerful, conscious commitment to participate with God in the healing process.

Continue to Work on Your Healing After Terminating Treatment

Personal growth does not have to stop just because your therapy sessions end. In fact, good therapy should teach you how to continue growing. We suggest that, as you end treatment, you set goals for yourself for the period that follows therapy. This will help you to "generalize" the insights and skills you have learned to new situations.

We could give many good examples of clients who have found this beneficial. For example, some clients continue to dedicate the therapy appointment time every week to their own personal reflection and growth. They pray, read helpful books, keep a journal, or meet regularly with a good friend to discuss areas of growth. There are many good ways to continue the growth process started in therapy.

Chapter 8

Terminating Psychotherapy

Because of the intense feelings that form as part of every psychotherapeutic relationship, saying good-bye to a therapist often elicits a strange mixture of feelings. It is not always as easy as it seems. Often one feels that it is like leaving home for the first time all over again. It's like saying good-bye to a good friend or like ending a romantic relationship or even a marriage. It is no wonder that both clients and therapists often find it very painful to let go.

When Should You Terminate?

The answer seems straightforward enough: When you've finished your therapy. In a perfect world, clients would not need to worry about when to end the therapy relationship. Therapists would monitor the course of therapy and end treatment when the appropriate time came. However, this is not a perfect world! In the real world it is difficult to know when to terminate treatment.

First, let us give some reasons *not* to terminate therapy. Never terminate therapy just because you are uncovering painful issues in your life or from your past. Often this is the point where many want to quit. But doing so is like jumping off the operating table just after the surgeon has opened up your abdomen to take out your appendix. You will be left with open wounds!

Also, don't abruptly quit because you don't think that you are making enough progress or that the changes you are making are too painful. We all feel this way at certain times.

Quitting because of anger towards your therapist is also quite common—and should be resisted. Instead, bring these feelings up with your therapist and talk about them. These can often be a sign that there is something else going on in the therapy which, when brought out into the open, is often a source of insight. Of course, if your therapist resists talking about your feelings, then your dissatisfaction and/or anger are a good indication that it is time to quit.

Finally, never quit just because someone else tells you to. Stand up for yourself. Take control of your own decisions and don't be bullied by a spouse, parent, boss, or friend into quitting unless you have a reason to.

Several signs can tell you when you have reached the point of termination:

- You may have a clear sense of what you need to do and feel you can continue on your own.
- You might find yourself being restless in therapy because it is not moving fast enough.
- You may not really have anything more you wish to talk about.

In each of these situations, the first thing to do is talk about your feelings of wanting to terminate with your therapist.

How Many Sessions?

Many people ask the question: How many sessions does it take to complete therapy or counseling? Unfortunately, this question is nearly impossible to answer. Both of us have dealt with problems where three or four sessions were all that was needed to resolve a crisis. On the other hand, Dr. Hart has had several clients on and off for more than fifteen years. "Maintenance" therapy is becoming more and more common because it prevents a relapse into a more serious condition. For example, someone prone to depression may find a visit to the therapist once every few months is very helpful in preventing slipping back into defeatist or depressive thinking patterns, and if such intermittent visits can prevent a more serious bout with depression, then it is well worth the effort. "Prevention is better than cure" is as true for mental health as it is for physical health!

While some people will benefit from as few as seven or eight sessions, others will require forty or fifty sessions before they begin to see the desired progress. Yet others may need to accept long-term therapy if the nature of the problem warrants it. The trauma of life can sometimes leave very deep scars that cannot be easily erased.

Will therapy itself indicate when it is time to terminate? The obvious time to stop therapy is when you have reached the goals you have set for yourself. On a positive note, you may wish to terminate treatment after you have built up some momentum and feel you can continue toward your goal on your own.

Reasons for Premature Termination

While the best reason for terminating therapy is that you have reached your stipulated goals for therapy, there are also, unfortunately, many instances when it is appropriate to end therapy prematurely because something else has happened to your relationship with your therapist which prevents you from reaching your goals.

In their extreme forms, the problem situations we will mention are often a sign that you are in "toxic therapy." Toxic therapy, rather than helping, is likely to cause you psychological harm. The sooner you recognize it and get out of therapy the better.

Indicator 1: Sexual Contact Between the Therapist and You

Any erotic or sexual contact between you and your therapist is always illegal and unethical. It makes no difference if both therapist and client are single, meet by chance at a social engagement outside of therapy, and believe you are "free" and "consenting" adults. It also does not matter if the therapist suggests that such contact will be therapeutically valuable. It will not. It is always wrong and damaging, and it is the responsibility of the therapist to prevent this contact from occurring. If you feel vulnerable here, it is time to say good-bye. If you have been approached sexually, you may contact the licensing board in your state; your therapist is acting in a grossly unethical manner and will likely face both ethical and criminal charges.

What is more, the responsibility for this behavior is wholly the therapist's. This abuse of power can trick and harm even the most well-intentioned clients.

Many clients and therapists who wish to have a social or romantic relationship end their therapeutic relationship so that they can feel comfortable dating. This is also unethical. In most states, clients and therapists are required to wait at least two years after therapy has ended before starting a dating or social relationship. Some states prohibit such a change entirely. The bottom line is that any romantic involvement between therapists and former clients is wrong, and should be avoided.

In addition to such obvious and overtly erotic or sexual contact between therapist and client, therapy can become sexualized to the detriment of the client in other ways. For example, therapy sessions might become excessively focused on sexual themes; client or therapist might take on a seductive interactional style; or client or therapist might start dressing in a provocative manner. Such behaviors often provide the possibility of significant personal insight and growth when properly talked about, worked through, and understood. However, if your therapist refuses to talk about such feelings or occurrences by denying them, defending them, or blaming you for them, you probably need to look elsewhere to continue your therapy.

Indicator 2: Gross "Dual Relationship" Violations

The concept of "dual relationship" is important to understand because many ethical rules that govern therapists are based on it.

Most professions place a taboo on all "dual relationships." As the phrase implies, a "dual relationship" means having more than one type of relationship at the same time, such as being a therapist and social friend, business partner, or especially a lover.

A friend once candidly asked me: "Isn't the therapeutic relationship strange?" I had to agree with him. Therapy is an unusual relationship. The relationship between client and therapist is typically intense and often involves very powerful, consequential feelings. One reason such feelings become possible in therapy (where they might not be possible in any other relationship) is because therapy provides a place of safety that is guaranteed by the structure of the therapy relationship. This structure and safety is often threatened by any parallel "non-therapeutic" relationship.

Because of this, a therapist and client should not attempt to maintain a second relationship, such as a friendship, or business arrangement. A therapist may not initiate a friendship with a client or even see a client socially outside of their therapy relationship. It will damage the therapeutic relationship mainly because the balance of power is in the therapist's favor. In a business arrangement the therapist could abuse this power for his or her own benefit.

It is also inappropriate for a therapist to do therapy with friends, or friends of his or her family.

While the prohibition of dual roles might not always make sense to lay people, it usually becomes clear when one considers what happens in practice. For example, a therapist who sees the spouse of a friend would create an uncomfortable and awkward situation if the two couples met in a social setting. How could the client express anger about her spouse (the therapist's friend)? This therapist would find himself in the "dual role" (friend and therapist), and could not be a friend to the husband and therapist to the wife at the same time. The therapist role demands total objectivity, and dual relationships violate one or other of the relationships.

Indicator 3: Breakdowns in Confidentiality

As a client you should feel absolutely assured that your therapist is not going to tell anyone else about you or your problems, unless you (1) give permission, or (2) if someone's life is in danger. This is called the "privilege of confidentiality" and is essential to good therapy.

Therapy requires that you feel the freedom to express feelings you wouldn't otherwise admit. You need to be assured that no one else will know these feelings or facts.

It is unethical and often illegal for your therapist to violate this confidence and divulge anything about your therapy to someone. Yet this occasionally happens.

If you were to hear that your therapist talked about you by name to other clients or friends, bring the issue to the attention of your therapist. If you conclude that your therapist has broken confidentiality, you should understand that this is a serious violation of your trust. You have the right to report your therapist to the licensing board in your state. You may want to determine whether or not you would benefit from additional sessions with this therapist. This decision would likely depend upon the nature of the information that was inappropriately shared.

Other violations in confidentiality may seem less severe. A therapist might casually mention an incident from your experience to a colleague or close family member. Such breaks in confidentiality may even have been done with good intentions, such as getting advice or supervision, or with a view to enlist prayer support. But it is still a violation of trust.

The bottom line is this: You—and you alone—are the one who determines who your therapist can talk to about your therapy. Your therapist has no choice but to follow your wishes. Otherwise, he or she is acting in an unethical and possibly criminal manner.

Indicator 4: "Toxic" Dependence

In an ideal world, therapy is effective because a client, whose life may have been full of painful or sinful experiences, unloving or damaging relationships, finally has the opportunity to change and develop a healthy and life-renewing relationship.

Unfortunately, as we have mentioned, this is not an ideal world. Instead, therapists and clients often get caught up in an unhealthy and dependent relationship to which they desperately cling, despite the obvious lack of progress on the part of the client.

A toxic dependency can arise due to psychological problems of either the therapist or the client, but usually it is a combination of both. Therapists and clients can often form an alliance of sorts, often unconsciously, that continues their unhealthy relationship. Why? Because it meets unhealthy needs.

Toxic therapy meets many unhealthy needs for the therapist. Some therapists have a need to feel needed, in control, or to be like a powerful parent. Such needs exploit the psychological vulnerability of the client. Sometimes emotionally immature clients find themselves in such a pathologically dependent relationship, because it gives them the false comfort of being totally taken care of, not unlike the way a small child feels toward his or her parents.

Such clients might enjoy being the center of attention, even if it is for just one hour per week and has no positive impact on the rest of their lives. Others never really consider making significant life changes. Instead, they enjoy psychotherapy because it provides sympathy for their emotional pain.

One can easily see how such relationships, formed out of unhealthy needs, become difficult to end. The therapist superficially feels needed, important, and in control. The client feels superficially loved and experiences a temporary relief of symptoms.

The end result is that toxic dependence between therapist and client leads to a never-ending therapy that does not promote healing. It can, in fact, be harmful.

Pathological dependence can also be subtle. Clients might find their therapist being overly sympathetic. So, rather than working to understand difficult feelings and finding effective solutions, they wallow in feelings of self pity. Or, the therapist lets go of his or her neutral position and joins the client in blaming people for problems. Neutrality on the part of a therapist is absolutely necessary to maintain a position of objectivity.

What are some of the signs that you are too dependent on your therapist?

- You have no goals of your own.
- You express mutual compliments every week.

- Your therapist sides with you against others, rather than helps you face up to and work through your problem relationships.
- You can make no major decisions without first discussing it with your therapist.
- Whenever your therapist goes away, you feel like you are about to fall apart.
- You have a need to see your therapist more often that your therapist deems necessary.

We want to sound another warning at this point. Toxic therapists play games to keep you in therapy. As you reach the end of your therapy goals, they invent other issues to keep you involved. In these times of economic hardship, many therapists are having difficulty staying in business. So be on guard against overly zealous therapists who would like to keep you in therapy forever!

When you do decide to end therapy, some therapists will continue to call you at home. They may rationalize the calls as a concern for your well-being, but it is always inappropriate for a therapist to do this unless you have given them permission to do so.

If your therapist strongly believes it is in your best interest to continue therapy, he or she may lay out the likely consequences of termination. However, far from telling you objectively what to expect, many therapists will make disparaging predictions about what is likely to happen if you end therapy without their approval. Still others might threaten to not see you again if you discontinue therapy. Such punitive responses will likely feel hurtful, but they indicate a very unsatisfactory therapist attitude. These responses are probably the surest signs that you are right in wanting to terminate.

Many people who wish to terminate against their therapists' wishes are confused about their real motives. That is, at times they feel good about terminating and think that the therapist might be manipulating them. Yet at other times they worry that they really might be avoiding deeper issues. What is more, their attempts to talk about this with their therapist have only left them more confused. In this situation we recommend finding a third person, either a good friend who is familiar with the process of therapy or another therapist, to help sort these issues out.

How to Leave Your Therapy

Throughout this section we have used the term "termination" as if it could be likened to an Arnold Schwarzeneggar-like encounter with a therapist: You say "hasta la vista, baby!" and boldly leave the office. However, this is usually not the way termination works. Termination typically takes at least three to four weeks to complete. During this process you and your therapist will look back over your therapy, identify areas of progress as well as non-progress, savor accomplishments, and honestly grieve areas of loss and unhealed psychological pain. You will look to the future and the problems that might be expected there.

Termination, like other leave-taking or separation experiences from your life, often elicits very powerful feelings, both positive and negative. These leave-takings, such as leaving home, the death of family members, or the loss of close relationships, often mold the way we relate to others. Termination offers the chance to re-experience these feelings, but this time with you in control. As a therapeutic experience, termination itself allows you to gain insight, work through, and understand issues of separation.

You can learn a lot about yourself in a short period of time here. Termination provides accelerated personal growth and insight. Therefore, it is extremely important that you do not just decide to terminate and not show up for any more appointments. Nor should you just storm out of the room. You need to consider several important issues to maximize the value of your termination:

1. Be honest with yourself and your therapist about why you are terminating. If you feel good about the goals you have accomplished, say so. If you are terminating because your therapy is about to uncover things that are too painful for you to handle at this stage in your life, be honest about this as well.

2. Review the progress of therapy and make efforts to summarize what you have learned. This is called "consolidation." Having clarified the goals you have achieved, you will likely find it helpful

to set new goals for personal growth to work toward after therapy has ended.

3. Termination is usually a wonderful time to express your genuine appreciation and your genuine frustration, anger, and disappointment in the relationship. It is important to leave therapy having been as honest as possible with your therapist, leaving little, if any, "unfinished business."

4. Clarify the nature of your relationship with your therapist once you have terminated. You may decide later that you would like to go back for an occasional checkup, so you need to know if this is possible. Similarly, you may later find yourself in a crisis and decide you want to discuss it with your therapist. So make sure you have a clear agreement about this with your therapist.

Don't be surprised if you find yourself missing your therapy after you have terminated. This is no reason to resume therapy, but if your experience in therapy has been a good one, the separation will naturally be somewhat painful. Accept this for what it is—a temporary period of grief. It will soon pass, like all grief, and you will be left with the progress you made in therapy, as well as many good feelings and happy memories about your therapist.

PART 3

Spiritual Direction

Chapter 9

Spiritual Direction in the Formation of Christian Character

In today's psychological culture, we are often more quick to seek out psychological help than spiritual direction. In fact, to most of us spiritual direction, if we've heard of it at all, is a new idea that remains fuzzy around the edges.

What exactly is spiritual direction? Or, as many have asked us, how different is the work of spiritual direction from other ministries, such as teaching, evangelizing, discipling, spiritual guidance, or just simple pastoral care?

Before we go any further, therefore, let us define what we mean by spiritual direction.

1. Spiritual direction focuses on the development of your relationship with God.

When I asked a well-known spiritual director recently to distinguish psychotherapy and spiritual direction, she told me that the difference is an easy one: "Spiritual direction is about developing one's relationship with God. We build this relationship with God through prayer. Therefore, if someone is not interested in developing a life of prayer, then we have nothing to talk about."

William Barry and William Connolly, two well-known and respected scholars who wrote a wonderful book entitled *The Practice of Spiritual Direction*, summed up their understanding of spiritual direction in the following statement:

> We define spiritual direction, then, as help given by one Christian to another which enables that person to pay attention to God's personal communication to him or her, to respond to this personally communicating God, to grow in intimacy with this God, and to live out the consequences of the relationship.[1]

This, of course, does not mean that spiritual direction does not address the entirety of a person's life, including relationships, stress, and problem behaviors. However, these personal aspects of life are discussed in a way that always keeps in the forefront the person's relationship with God.

At its best, spiritual direction helps to transform our understanding of Jesus. He moves from being a historical figure to becoming a real friend. The Jesus of history becomes the Jesus of our personal biographies.

2. Spiritual direction helps you discern God's guidance in your life.

As Christians we must not only know in theory the difference between good and evil, but we also must be able to identify good from bad and right from wrong. This process of discerning good from evil is a gift given by the Spirit (1 Corinthians 12:7) and central to spiritual direction.

Often, however, we need to make decisions that are not clearly "good" or "evil." For example, my (Dr. Hogan's) pastor once asked me to chair a committee at church. At first I felt good about the prospect of doing this work. Then, after reflection, I considered the negative consequences it might have on my relationship with my family and on my work with clients. My decision was not a question of good or evil, but a question of where God most would want me to spend my time and talents.

Discerning God's direction even in life's minor decisions is one important focus of spiritual direction.

3. Spiritual direction helps us see how God works in everyday, ordinary situations.

Most of us have been discipled by spiritual teachers who have greatly helped us to learn new ideas about God. This can often be an exciting process. However, most of us at some point become frustrated by the difficulties we have applying our insights to our everyday life. This can leave us feeling as though we are leading two entirely different lives—our life of ideas about God, and our everyday life of activities, habits, and struggles. Spiritual direction aims at joining our ideas about God to real-world circumstances and life events. It helps to answer important questions: How is God present in this difficulty at work? How might God be calling me to grow through this conflict with my wife? This process transforms the general events of our lives into personal, meaningful events centered on the work of a personal God in our midst.

Spiritual direction also helps us to identify our talents and gifts and shows us how to use them to advance the kingdom of God. One person may find that she has the gift of leadership and administration, and therefore choose to administrate the Sunday school program instead of teaching a class. Another person may find that he loves to be with elderly people most, and therefore choose a career that allows him to minister to them. Spiritual direction helps us to understand, in practical ways, how our natural interests and abilities can be used for the glory of God, both in our work lives and in our church lives.

A Brief History of Spiritual Direction

This, no doubt, sounds like an exciting ministry to encounter! Most of us would love to increase our awareness of God's presence. Yet not too long ago the idea of spiritual direction was totally foreign to most Christians.

However, spiritual direction is nothing new! The seeds of spiritual direction can be traced back to the New Testament when John and Paul recognized that Christians would also need to grow in discernment (Philippians 1:9–10) and help each other to test the spirits (1 John 4:1).

In the early days of the church, Christians received spiritual guidance simply from participating in the life of the church. They celebrated the Lord's Supper, confessed their sins, and talked to one another about prayer and the spiritual life freely. God was real and close, and talk about God as natural as breathing.

This situation changed as small groups, in an attempt to live a more pure and godly life, moved away from established churches into the desert. There they found the going rough: temptation and trials occurred, and the will of God became less evident. They required help in their efforts to test the spirits and to continue their growth in knowledge and discernment. In this atmosphere, they sought the counsel of older and wiser Christians, who were called "spiritual fathers." By the third and fourth centuries, even religious leaders from the villages made their way to the desert to seek the direction of these mature, prayerful, and well-respected men and women.

Spiritual direction became an activity done primarily by priests and religious leaders for other priests and religious leaders. Few lay people even knew much about spiritual direction. In other words, spiritual direction came to be a ministry which was carried on only by religious "professionals."

This attitude of "leaving it to the professionals" had its good points and produced some substantial rewards. For instance, these professionals took their work seriously! In addition to ongoing spiritual direction which occurred in one-on-one relationships, spiritual experiences were studied, organized, analyzed, and committed to writing. These writings helped to bring a logical clarity to the Christian faith which was not penetrable by secular philosophy. Many of these treasures of the life of the church remain largely underappreciated to this day.[2]

However, all this formalization of the Christian faith also had its pitfalls. Those involved became autocratic. As church leaders began to teach a single best way to know and experience God, many in the church became uncomfortable and resentful of their tactics.

This resentment was at the heart of the Protestant reformation. Protestants wanted to take a different direction toward spirituality. They called it "pietism," which emphasized "heart religion," strict morality, holiness, and the priesthood of all believers. This new approach to religion found little value in taking direction from authority figures such as spiritual directors.

Meanwhile, most Catholics were also going without spiritual direction, but for different reasons. Catholic spirituality came to focus almost exclusively on the sacraments for spiritual experience and development. Thus, the activity of spiritual direction was largely limited to priests and other Christian leaders.

To suggest that Protestants and Roman Catholics have been without any spiritual direction over the past six centuries would be misleading, however. In fact, both have benefited from ministries closely related to spiritual direction; namely, Catholic "confession" and Protestant "discipleship" or "spiritual formation."

The general lack of interest in spiritual direction in much of the Christian church has now radically changed. Believers in this post-modern and post-Christian era are showing a tremendous thirst to develop an individual, Christian spirituality that can withstand the forces of disintegration and destruction that mark this period in history.

The world is changing at an extremely rapid pace. Many institutions that have long guided Christians, such as families, neighborhood communities, and church communities, are breaking down. Old traditions are disintegrating. Many people are lost and at the mercy of life's uncertainties.

This is just the state of confusion that is ripe for the remedial work of spiritual direction. An anchor in a storm-tossed world, spiritual direction can often be more effective in restoring meaning to life than any amount of psychotherapy!

Who Benefits from Spiritual Direction?

As we have already mentioned, leaders in the church often seek out and benefit from spiritual direction. Priests and pastors depend on this ministry to help them discern where the Holy Spirit is leading them and their church community. Many Protestant pastors, for instance, now use a spiritual director to help them cope with burnout and stress. However, more and more people from all walks of life have now begun to see the benefits of spiritual direction.

Is this a good thing? Should everyone who is serious about pursuing God pursue spiritual direction? If not, who should pursue spiritual direction?

To begin with, we believe anyone who feels led by the Holy Spirit to enter spiritual direction should do so! It is not a benefit reserved only for pastors or priests. God's prompting is the first and most important indication that you will likely benefit from intentional direction. However, other indicators could point to spiritual direction as a fruitful experience.

First, people tend to benefit from spiritual direction if they are not satisfied with the status quo and feel a longing to grow. Such people long for a deeper awareness of their spiritual side and of God.

This raises an interesting question. Don't all Christians feel this way? No, they don't. Our experience of the diversity of the church suggests that not all Christians, even good Christians, feel this way. Some are quite content with their spiritual experience even though it doesn't appear to have a lot of depth. They know their limitations and live godly lives to the best of their abilities. For others, however, this is not enough. They long for a deeper experience of God's fullness.

Second, people tend to benefit from spiritual direction if they are capable of and desire to be in deeper social relationships. The relationship between the director and the directee is the ground within which the work of direction takes place. Therefore, people who, for any reason, have difficulty engaging in interpersonal relationships might have great difficulty with spiritual direction.

Other than these two qualifications, we see no others that would limit who would benefit from spiritual direction.

In addition to those who are likely to benefit, there are others whom we commonly recommend for spiritual direction. Anyone in ministry positions should make spiritual direction a high priority.

We believe spiritual leaders and pastors will derive a definite benefit, particularly during times of difficulty. Similarly, those with a special or limited vocation in the church often find spiritual direction beneficial as well.

Those preparing for or going through a major transition are also likely to benefit from spiritual direction. Thus, college students trying to decide on a career, young adults who are considering marriage, and adults who might be coping with some ongoing adversity, would all be good candidates for a fruitful period of spiritual direction.

Issues in Spiritual Direction

Spiritual directors tend to look most closely at (1) how you practice Christian spirituality and (2) how your spirituality has developed over time.

Christian Spirituality

Christian spirituality is a term used to describe how people communicate openly and personally with God, as well as how this relationship with God guides the way they live in the world. It includes such practices as prayer, singing, meditation, Bible study, Christian service, corporate worship, and so on.

Much has been written about how different people experience God in different ways based on their own personalities or temperament. This knowledge is often essential in unlocking Christians from their spiritual desert.

Not long ago a woman came to see me (Dr. Hogan) who was feeling very guilty for using a meditation technique typically considered non-Christian. As I spoke with her further, I learned that she had been a Christian for many years but found herself exceedingly anxious. She gained little consolation in her study of the Bible. A friend had taught her some mind tricks to help her meditate, which were part of a non-Christian spiritual tradition. But when she went to her pastor, she was told such mind focusing was a spiritually dangerous practice.

This woman felt emotionally torn: She could either continue in a Christian practice—Bible study—that had long since dried up, or she could pursue a supposedly "dangerous" practice that gave her peace. Her spiritual director, however, helped her to discover Christian forms of meditation which had a long and solid history in the church. For her, this meditation was not only comfortable, but seemed to open her to the ministering of the Holy Spirit.

This woman's problem was not a lack of faith or love for God. Her problem was that her limited understanding of Christian spirituality kept her from experiencing God in a way that took into consideration her personality. By learning more about different Christian spiritual practices, she was able to recommit to her faith in a way that worked for her personality.

Many Christians have historically focused on just one or another spiritual practice, leaving those with a different style to conclude that the Christian faith cannot be pursued. We often meet people who are entrenched in daily psychological abuse because they have irregular, dry, and empty quiet times studying Scripture. Further exploration with such folks often reveals that they continue to pray and/or study the Bible using the exact same one or two ways they were taught as children. When these forms of prayer stop working, they conclude that God is no longer accessible or that they are defective and can no longer access God. A spiritual director helps people to understand their personality, assess their spiritual practices, and recommend practices that will help them grow in their Christian life.

Spiritual Development

Human beings are constantly growing physically, mentally, and spiritually. Physicians monitor the growth, development, and maturity of the human body. Psychologists monitor and measure the growth, development, and maturity of the cognitive, emotional, and relational functioning. And spiritual directors monitor the growth, development, and maturity of the spirit.

Paul knew this lesson well. He advised Timothy to keep new converts away from active ministry as elders because he knew that these pressures might cause them to lead poorly (1 Timothy 3:6). Paul recognized his own development process when he wrote: "When I was a child, I talked like a child, I thought like a child, I reasoned like a child. When I became a man, I put childish ways behind me" (1 Corinthians 13:11).

The spiritual life of Christians changes over time. Consequently, what might be meaningful to the new convert might seem dry, empty, or clichéd to the spiritually mature. Spiritual directors understand how spirituality changes over time and can use this knowledge to understand the maturity of a Christian's relationship with God.

In their book *The Critical Journey*, Janet Hagberg and Robert Guelick provide an outline of the typical stages of faith:

Stage 1: The Recognition of God. A sense of awe of who God is and our need for him.

Stage 2: The Life of Discipleship. Beginning to learn the ways of God and how they relate to life's challenges.

Stage 3: The Productive Life. Consciously working for God in communal life.

Stage 4: The Journey Inward. The understanding of the deeper inner experiences of God—unsettling but healing.

Stage 5: The Journey Outward. After discovering a new wholeness at the deep inner level, the working out of faith with humility and confidence.

Stage 6: The Life of Love. Reflecting God to others in the world, more consistently and with less human effort.

A spiritual director will never hurry you through a stage of development, but will help you recognize where you are and help you to grow to the next stage in your spiritual life.

Forms of Spiritual Direction

As spiritual direction has increased in popularity, its forms have multiplied. The most common form of spiritual direction is the traditional one. The director meets with one person, usually once every four to eight weeks. The advantage to this form of direction is that you can often take the time you need to explore and relate all the issues you wish. A personal spiritual friendship can develop in this type of direction.

However, this one-one-one relationship is not always possible. Effective spiritual directors are often in great demand and unable to give direction to everyone who requests it. Other forms of direction have, therefore, emerged.

One of these new forms is group direction. In this setting a spiritual director meets with a group of four to six persons at a time, giving most of the direction. The advantage to this approach is that you often learn about the working of the Holy Spirit by listening to the ways the Spirit is working in the lives of others. The disadvantage is also obvious: You have less time to focus on your own issues and the setting is less private.

Another form is mutual spiritual direction. As the name implies, the direction is given mutually between two or more people who take turns at being the director. In this approach, Christians get together without anyone being the spiritual director. They provide mutual direction to each other.

This is not unlike a traditional prayer group which has no specific leader, except that the purpose here is the discernment of the work of the Holy Spirit in the lives of group members. The advantage to this is that the spiritual director's influence is limited. However, the lack of a clear leader can be detrimental. Without having someone who is trained to handle the responsibility of spiritual direction, a group often loses a sense of accountability. In addition, group dynamics or conflicts are often difficult to manage without a facilitator. If two people find themselves angry with each other, the group could disintegrate.

Other forms of spiritual direction are continuing to evolve. Most are based on matching the needs of both directors and directees. Concentrated retreats for spiritual direction, either once or several times a year, are popular with people who have busy lives and cannot give regular monthly time to the direction.

Since the goal of spiritual direction is to establish a relationship with a spiritual director, whatever way seems to work for both the director and directee is acceptable. There are no hard and fast rules. Be prepared to explore several options and open yourself to a fuller experience of God's Holy Spirit.

Chapter 10

Characteristics of a Good Spiritual Director

"How is your heart?"

Pastor John always started our spiritual direction meetings in the same way. A man of deep prayer, his words often cut through my restless and chaotic frame of mind, creating a stillness in the room which prepared us both for the task of spiritual direction. Like an experienced detective, he would gently examine my life experience—the joys, sorrows, treasures, and burdens—searching for evidence of God's challenges, grace, and redemption. Pastor John had a single-minded passion to rouse an awareness of God's presence that led to a deeper communion. I always left his office awakened to the presence of God's in my everyday circumstances.

Pastor John is an example of a spiritual director par excellence!

Personal Characteristics of a Good Spiritual Director

Where can you find a "Pastor John"? How will you recognize him or her? We would like to suggest that the following four characteristics should be evident in the life of any spiritual director.

1. Good spiritual directors are men and women of prayer.

Since one of the major goals of spiritual direction is to foster a personal life of prayer, a spiritual director must have developed a personal prayer life that is both disciplined and enriching. Nowhere is the adage that you "cannot teach a student more than you know yourself" truer than in the area of personal prayer.

Since prayer is such a personal and private matter, the quality of a spiritual director's prayer life is not always easy to discern. You may, therefore, need to address this matter forthrightly with someone you are considering as a director. Fortunately, a director will display a commitment to prayer in many ways: It shows itself by a willingness to pray frequently with you, by an attitude of dependence on prayer, and by the obvious fruits of a rich prayer life: love, joy, peace, patience, kindness, goodness, and self-control.

2. *Good spiritual directors understand that their work is a gift of the Holy Spirit, confirmed by the Christian community.*

Good spiritual directors receive their motivation to minister from their calling; it is a God-inspired talent or gift. Good spiritual directors also live their lives in active participation with the Christian community, where this calling is affirmed and confirmed. You should be wary, therefore, of those who put themselves forward as spiritual directors without the confirmation of the Christian community. Such people may be abusing what spiritual gifts they have.

The problem of misunderstood and abused spiritual gifts is nothing new. The church in Corinth, for instance, had members who were confused about their spiritual calling and attempted to exercise spiritual gifts as a way of seeking status over others. To remedy this, Paul proposed that gifts only be exercised in interdependent relationship with the body of Christ (1 Corinthians 12:12–30), and in selfless love (1 Corinthians 13).

Good spiritual directors, then, are those who are in a humble, committed relationship with the body of Christ. Thus the tradition of spiritual direction emphasizes that good spiritual directors must always be in a relationship with the Christian community and must also have either their own spiritual director or a supervisor for the ministry they do.

3. Good spiritual directors are personally mature.

Spiritual directors must be spiritually mature. You can never take a person further along the road of spiritual maturity than you yourself have traveled.

The spiritual life has many pitfalls and difficulties, many highs and lows. There are times when prayer is rich and times when it is dry, when God feels very close and when he feels very distant. Good spiritual directors are those who have been through many such cycles, who know what to anticipate, who know their patterns and how faith grows through them. I would hate to take a journey into a jungle led by a guide who has never been that way himself!

4. Good spiritual directors are mentally healthy and capable of forming lasting human relationships.

Spiritual direction usually occurs in the context of a confidential relationship between two people. If spiritual direction is going to be effective, the spiritual director must be capable of sustaining a fairly intimate relationship with the directee over a long period of time.

The relationship between spiritual director and directee often elicits powerful feelings in both the director and directee. Exploring the ways God works in the world involves a dialogue about that which is closest to our hearts. Our deepest and darkest secrets are brought into the light in shared communion. This relationship, then, often creates strong and alternating feelings of despair, joy, ecstasy, and hopelessness. The ability to manage and not be sucked into such overpowering feelings requires good mental health on the part of the director. Spiritual directors must be able to hear such feelings without taking them personally.

As with psychotherapy, erotic or sexual feelings on the part of director, directee, or both can easily develop when opposite sexes are involved, or if one or the other has latent and unresolved homosexual feelings. Spiritual directors need to have worked through these issues themselves so as to have the ability to recognize and work with these feelings effectively.

Education and Training of Spiritual Directors

Up to this point we have emphasized what a spiritual director should be, and we cannot emphasize these important personal characteristics enough! The ability to mentor another person in the ways of the Spirit is a gift given and a calling received; it cannot be engineered just by being a high-minded intellectual type who happens to work in a religious institution. However, we also know that the supernatural gifts of God often need to be exercised and developed before they can reach their full potential. Or, to put it another way, God does not only call the competent; he makes competent those he has called!

To become competent a spiritual director must receive structured education and training to learn the ways of God. The apostle Paul often reminded his own directees to be aware of false teaching and to remind themselves of the truth as previously taught (1 Timothy 4:1–6). Only the arrogant and ungodly think they can come to the truth all by themselves and ignore what Scripture teaches (1 Corinthians 4:18–19). Our world is full of people who think God is working in them, when in reality some other psychological, social, or spiritual force is at work.

Therefore, discerning the truth requires a foundation of knowledge gained by studying and training. Consider the words of Luke explaining why he committed his gospel to writing:

> Therefore, since I myself have carefully investigated everything from the beginning, it seemed good also to me to write an orderly account for you, most excellent Theophilus, so that you may know the certainty of the things you have been taught. (Luke 1:3–4)

Luke does not pretend that, when it comes to knowing the ways of God, he can just go into some meditative trance and come up with an understanding of how God works. Rather, he uses good, old-fashioned hard work and research.

In studying Scripture and the history of spiritual direction, we have determined three areas of training necessary to spiritual direction: knowledge of Scripture, basic theology, and Christian spirituality.

1. Knowledge of Scripture

The ultimate source for all information about the Christian life is the Bible. Yet the Bible is often sorely neglected. Even Christian leaders are often caught up in the latest popular Christian book or theological trend, and it never occurs to them to test what they have read by their primary text: Scripture.

We believe that anyone not steeped in what Scripture has to say about the spiritual life is not wholly able to provide effective spiritual direction. Scripture must always remain the primary source of information.

We draw attention to this to caution you against spiritual directors who have traded their Bible for the writings of unsound spiritual leaders or even unsound theology. As we are about to explain, familiarity with theology and with the great spiritual writers of the church is important, and even central to the training of a spiritual director. However, Scripture itself must always be the primary guide to the trustworthy spiritual director.

2. Knowledge of Basic Theology

In addition to a spiritual director's familiarity with Scripture, he or she should also be familiar with the theology developed from it. The term *theology* often leaves a bad taste in the mouth of Christians because of the tendency on the part of theologians to overanalyze God and his Word. However, when used in proper relationship with Scripture and with the proper attitude, theology is simply, in St. Augustine's words, "faith seeking understanding."

Familiarity with theology is also important because it helps us to discern and understand the specific sins of our culture in ways not readily apparent to those without such training. For example, the church has, at different times, endorsed ideas or movements that were more a reflection of individual or social evil than an honest interpretation of God's Word. For example, many Christian writers have written in support of anti-Semitism, slavery, racism, and the oppression of the poor. However, solid theological critique has helped the church to reject these false teachings. Any potential spiritual director who is not familiar with such study and writings is prone to repeat these mistakes.

Through theological study, then, spiritual directors learn to think clearly about God, and learn how God has been misunderstood through the ages. This prepares the spiritual director to guide and to discern the images and thoughts about God brought by the directee.

3. Knowledge of Christian Spirituality

Many things in the spiritual realm are not negotiable. For example, we cannot save ourselves and must accept the salvation won on Calvary; there is only one God who desires a relationship with his people; and sin is real and must be addressed if we are to have a genuine and vital relationship with Christ. These are the basics.

However, other aspects of our walk with Christ seem to be different depending on the person and culture he or she is in. Some Christians seek and experience God's presence via highly enthusiastic music, spiritual dancing, and speaking in tongues. Others know Christ through long hours of contemplative prayer and meditation. New converts often experience God as primarily interested in moral purity, while those who have walked in the faith for many years might be overwhelmed by the presence of the Holy Spirit in all things. Yet all Christians experience the same God.

If you were to read through the life of the saints, you would find the same diversity of experiences with God. These different experiences of the same God have led to the study of Christian spirituality. Competent spiritual directors are familiar with these various traditions of spirituality. Whether their familiarity comes from their own personal experience and reading or through formal education is unimportant. Familiarity with the various forms and traditions of Christian spirituality allows the spiritual director to understand more deeply what Christian spirituality looks like and how it develops over time.

Many "spiritual" practices currently popular, even in Christian circles with Christian-sounding names, have no or few scriptural roots. Instead, many of these were developed outside of the Christian faith, then "baptized" into the faith in the spirit of New Age philosophy or even ecumenism.

Our point is this: Without some knowledge of the distinctives of Christian spiritual development, a spiritual director might be prone to deception. This deception might feel good, comfortable, and religious. But in the end it might lead the believer and the director further from God, not closer. Therefore, a background in spirituality is not enough. Christians need spiritual directors with a background in *Christian* spirituality.

Potential Abuses in Spiritual Direction

The boom in the work of spiritual direction is good news!

However, like most good things, there is a flip side: Along with the rapid increase of sound, godly spiritual direction, there has also been an increase in cheap imitations of spiritual direction. While these counterfeit forms promise "spiritual growth," they typically deliver fleeting pleasant feelings at best, and at worst spiritual confusion. Needless to say, such activities offer little or no benefit to the development of Christian character.

One large area of abuse has been with the spiritual direction given outside of the Christian church. These spiritual directors, while seemingly good and harmless, wreak havoc on the inner life of Christians because of their confused understanding of the word *spiritual*. For these well-meaning folks, almost any type of experience, from watching a sunset to prancing around a fire, is interpreted as "spiritual." This abuse robs the term *spiritual* of its original meaning. It would be better if these other deeply pleasant or moving experiences would be called something else, so that *spiritual* could refer only to that which pertains to the spirit.

Participation in such practices also gives people the *feeling* that they are spiritual, momentarily numbing the thirst of the human soul for God without providing life-giving drink! And, while this can often lead participants to conclude that they are "being spiritual" (which is quite popular, even in psychological circles!), it causes severe malnutrition of the human soul.

The imitators of spiritual direction are usually outside mainline Christian circles. As such, they can be easily avoided by following a simple principle: If you are looking for solid spiritual guidance and direction, stay close to the body of Christ!

Conclusion

St. John of the Cross refers to untrained and ineffective spiritual helpers as "a major obstacle to spiritual progress, even worse than the devil himself." Strong words! Spoken, no doubt, out of personal experience. Such warnings remind us that defective spiritual direction might actually harm our relationship with God.

The best way to ensure that you get sound spiritual direction is to make sure you choose a sound and healthy spiritual director, with all the characteristics we have outlined in this chapter. In the next chapter, we share with you the steps for finding a good spiritual director.

Chapter 11

Steps to Getting Good Spiritual Direction

If you discern God's call for you to pursue the deeper development of your spiritual life through spiritual direction, approach the process of selection in a prayerful, organized, and systematic way. As we have already pointed out in several places throughout this book, the effectiveness of your development depends very much on the appropriate fit between you and your director, just as it does in psychotherapy between you and your therapist. The challenge is to find a spiritual director who is not only good, but also good for *you*. To find a good, competent, reliable, and personable spiritual director, we suggest that you follow these five steps:

1. Prepare yourself for the search.

Finding a spiritual director can be a long and at times trying process. You should prepare for it to take some time and to be frustrating at certain points, but you can do several things to make it easier.

First, keep your search focused in your prayers. This seems obvious. Who would want to pursue spiritual formation and yet not take time to pray about it? But it can happen. One can have a hunger for deeper spiritual experiences yet not have the strength or ability to engage in meaningful prayer. Those who are hungry don't always have the patience to pray for food. They just go and find it!

We cannot emphasize enough, though, the importance of prayer when pursuing something that has obvious implications for the kingdom of God. The temptation is to rely on one's own abilities, merits, and sensitivities. Yet it is exceptionally important that you attend to the development of your spiritual sensitivity so that you can discern the fit of those you interview. Praying increases spiritual sensitivity. It also helps you to slow down and listen to your feelings and what God is trying to say to you.

Second, prayerfully ponder what characteristics you would expect to be helpful in your spiritual director. Spiritual directors come in many different styles. Some are quiet and unassuming; others are gregarious and energetic. Some are friendly and open; others are quiet and even shy. They may all be fantastic directors but different in their style, and not all styles will suit you. You need to have some idea about what will work for you. Should you find someone who is the opposite of you? The same as you? What degree of compatibility should there be, or should you intentionally be incompatible to force yourself to be more tolerant of interpersonal tensions? Pray about these issues. God will show you the way!

Third, prepare yourself for a process that will require patience. The search for a director could be the first lesson God has in mind for your curriculum of growth. It might take several weeks, months, or even years before you find a spiritual director with whom you feel comfortable. Remember, your spiritual development started when you began searching, so use the search as the focus for your growth right from the start.

2. Establish your options for spiritual direction.

The first step here is to gather as many names of individuals and institutions who offer spiritual direction as you possibly can. The most obvious place to start is with your pastor. Depending on your denomination, as well as the type of person your pastor is, you can expect several possible responses when you approach your pastor with your request. First, your pastor may not be familiar with the field of spiritual direction. In many quarters it is seldom talked about. In a few there might even be a lot of suspicion towards it simply because it is not a part of your church's heritage. You may need, therefore, to suggest that your pastor read about spiritual direction. This book may be a good starting place. In a few cases, however, your pastor may be totally opposed to your looking into spiritual direction, in which case you will have to look for help elsewhere. Not that we would encourage mutiny, but there comes a time when you have to decide whether you are in the right place for your soul's sake.

A more hopeful sign is when your pastor feels that he or she would be the best person to provide your spiritual direction. Many pastors see the work of spiritual direction as one of the primary ministries they provide for their church community. However, even if your pastor is suitable, time is always a critical factor in ministry. Most clergy are eaten up by time and seldom can be available on a regular basis for more than just a few people. A few won't be able to say no to your request, so you might want to be considerate even before posing the request that the pastor be your director.

For a few people, the role of the pastor is not compatible with the role of spiritual director. They fear that their personal story might end up as a sermon illustration. It happens! They prefer a more confidential relationship with a director they don't have to relate to on committees or boards. Role conflicts can be a serious problem for pastors. If you anticipate that your pastor will want to be your spiritual director, but you do not want him or her to take on this role in your life, then you might consider going elsewhere for a recommendation.

A second place to look is in your church's programs. Many churches are now offering an occasional class on spirituality. Of course, such a course can take many forms. For some it may be nothing more than a Bible study, but for many it increasingly has a genuine spiritual formation or direction focus. If you perceive that the class is not oriented toward spiritual direction, you may want to propose to the leader that a program of intentional spiritual direction be considered. The leader may welcome such a forthright request.

It may be all the encouragement he or she is waiting for to launch such a program!

A third place to look for spiritual directors is in a local retreat house or center. For Catholics this is usually easy, but for Protestants it may be a little more difficult. Since finding a retreat house or center can sometimes be a little tricky (they have retreated from the world quite effectively), here are a few suggestions.

Retreat houses are often located outside of major metropolitan areas and are therefore not normally listed in the city section of a telephone book. So what can you do? First, contact the regional head office of your church denomination for recommendations. Second, call the head office of another denomination that you believe might have a retreat center. If you still have not found what you are looking for, call large churches in your community and ask if they know the whereabouts of any retreat houses. Finally, write to Retreats International, Box 1067, Notre Dame, IN 46556, and ask if they can provide a listing of retreat houses in your area. They are a wonderful resource and are always happy to help people looking for a retreat house. They may ask you for a nominal donation to cover the costs of mailing the list. Once you have the numbers of a few retreat houses, call and ask them for information about additional local retreat houses. Retreat houses do not typically compete with each other like businesses, so they should help you compile a good list of possibilities.

A fourth place to contact is a local monastery. If you are Protestant and not sure if you should do this, let us assure you that many Protestant clergy, even the very conservative ones, take advantage of the facilities offered at Catholic monasteries for either personal spiritual retreats or for spiritual direction. Whatever your theology, you can be assured that no one is going to interfere with it. If they do, get out immediately. They don't deserve your business. I (Dr. Hart) am thoroughly Protestant, evangelical, and conservative in my theology, but some of the most uplifting times I have ever experienced were in retreat with other pastors in an Abbey, observing the devotion and worship of the inhabitants.

Monasteries commonly have people around who are willing to do spiritual direction. Sometimes you may also stay overnight in these monasteries for a nominal donation. You can then combine a retreat with a visit to your spiritual director.

3. Explore and screen options and settings.

Once you have created a long list of potential spiritual directors, let your fingers do the walking and put your telephone to good use. Your goal in this step is to narrow your list of spiritual directors to those who are both likely and available to help you. There are several important questions to ask at this stage:

- Is a director currently available to do spiritual direction?
- What hours and days is he or she available?
- Is there a fee? If so, how much? If there is no fee, how is he or she financially supported?
- What is this director's general history and background in spiritual direction? Number of years of experience? What training has he or she received?
- Are there groups of people that this spiritual director prefers to work with, such as Catholics, women, men, pastors, or church leaders, etc.?
- Is this spiritual director involved in retreat work?

After you have answers to these questions, we recommend that you narrow your list of potential spiritual directors down to two or three. You are then ready to schedule a first interview with each.

4. Interview prospective spiritual directors.

Before you commit to any long-term relationship with a spiritual director, you will want to spend a little time getting to know him or her to find out if there is a natural fit. Most spiritual directors will want to determine this too.

We would recommend that you ask the spiritual director whatever questions you feel are important. Of course, spiritual directors may decide not to answer all of your questions, particularly if your questions probe their personal lives. Like psychotherapists, they are entitled to a degree of anonymity.

Be sure to cover the following areas in your inquiries: who "authorizes" this person to do spiritual direction, formal background and training, value commitments, personal maturity, interpersonal skills, and logistics of meeting.

Authorization

Ask: Are you ordained, set apart for a special ministry, or on staff? How did you get started doing spiritual direction? How do you see your role in the larger church and the kingdom of God? Look for the degree to which this person came to spiritual direction out of a "calling" versus out of merely wanting some personal gratification; a sense that this person sees his or her work as flowing from the work of the Holy Spirit, rather than out of his or her own expertise.

Formal Background and Training

Ask: What kind of background reading and training have you had? Is there a writer, ancient or modern, in the church for whom you have a particular affinity? What role do you see Scripture taking in spiritual direction? Look for a healthy respect for the formal training that helps to form spiritual directors: a familiarity with Scripture, theology, and Christian spirituality.

Value Commitments

Ask: Are you part of a Christian community? Does this have a connection to the work we will do? What does it mean for a person to be "godly," "healthy," and/or "holy"? What does good spiritual direction look like to you? Are you committed to a life of faith or the kingdom of God? Look for a vital relationship with the church community; basic agreement on any issue which is important to you; whether the overall world view of this person seems godly and attractive. As with psychotherapists, spiritual directors often talk about questions without answering them. This might simply indicate a desire to understand your concern, not to avoid the answer.

Personal Maturity

Ask: Do you receive supervision in your spiritual direction or have you had spiritual direction yourself? Do you still receive ongoing spiritual direction? If you and I were to get stuck, will you go to another professional for help? Look for an openness to talk about these issues and a lack of defensiveness. Ask yourself if this person is hiding behind his or her role more than you are comfortable with. Honesty and openness are essential characteristics for a good spiritual director.

Interpersonal Skills

Since the work of spiritual direction is very personal, a high level of interpersonal competence is necessary. After you leave the spiritual director's office, ask yourself: Did you feel respected? Did you feel accepted? Did the spiritual director seem comfortable with you, or was he or she threatened? Did you feel comfortable or threatened?

Logistics of Meeting

Ask: How often are you able to meet? Would it be possible to increase our frequency of meeting if needed? What kind of fee would you like me to pay you? Who do I pay it to? If there is no fee, can I make a donation? To whom should the donation go? Practical matters pertaining to money are best handled frankly and openly.

Look for logistical problems that might get in the way of obtaining the spiritual direction you need and want.

5. Prayerfully reflect upon each spiritual director you interviewed.

Once you have gone through each of these steps and clarified the objective qualifications as well as the interpersonal match between you and each spiritual director, take some time to pray again over your decision. After all, you are making a major investment of time here, if not money. Give time to prayerfully discern which person is likely to be most beneficial in your quest for spiritual growth. Try to avoid the temptation to rush into direction. You should take whatever time you need. You will know when you are ready. There will be a comfortable sense of confidence that the spiritual director you have chosen is the one most likely to help you.

Should There Be a Fee for Spiritual Direction?

A common question has to do with whether a spiritual director should charge a fee. Some think that spiritual directors, like other counselors, should charge for their services. Others feel that the church should provide spiritual direction as a part of its ministry, and "I've already paid my dues there!"

We believe that the bottom line is that all healers have to be supported in one way or another. In our world there is no other way to provide such services. While spiritual directors have traditionally not charged for their services because they were generously supported by the church, not all churches now fund such programs themselves, just as they don't all fund counseling services. Christian psychologists and counselors have typically not received direct financial support from the church and have therefore typically charged for their services.

Therefore, if you can find a spiritual director who is supported by the church you may end up not having to pay a fee. But you cannot expect such a blessing in all circumstances. Churches also suffer when the economy is down. It's not that churches don't care; they can only stretch a dollar so far. If you cannot find a spiritual director who receives financial support from a church, you may have to pay for the services.

Conclusion

There is the possibility that no matter how hard you try, you are not able to locate a spiritual director. What should you do? Abandon your quest? Put it on hold for a while? Settle for someone who is second best?

Obviously, this is a decision you must make for yourself. But there is one further suggestion we would make. While it is not the preferred way, since spiritual direction works best when there is accountability built into the discipline, one can go it alone.

If you have genuinely tried without success to find a spiritual director, then you may have to trust God to guide you along, at least until you can find a director. If you have a friend or spouse who will share the journey with you, you might find the encouragement to be more fulfilling.

Our main point is this: If you really hunger for a deeper experience of God, don't put off that quest. Spiritual hunger cannot be delayed. You must respond to it. God knows this and will provide you with a way to fulfill your search.

Since many books are available on the topic of spiritual formation and direction, we would encourage you to use this resource. Choose from the suggested reading list we provide at the end of this book. Set up a regular reading schedule and learn all you can. It isn't easy, we know, but God will honor your quest.

If you can read a book out loud with someone else and then take time to discuss what you have read, you will find it more meaningful than if you just read it silently to yourself. We lost something very precious when we invented silent reading a couple of hundred years ago—the value of sharing ideas out loud with each other. Spiritual formation cannot take place in silence and in the deep recesses of your mind. It needs to be talked about, shared, and mutually experienced if it is going to be maximally beneficial. A blessing hoarded is a blessing canceled! A blessing shared is a blessing multiplied! It is not without reason that we are told: "Bear ye one another's burdens, and so fulfill the law of Christ" (Galatians 6:2).

Chapter 12

Psychology and Spiritual Direction: Bringing the Two Together

In the previous chapters we have made an effort to clarify the differences between spiritual direction and psychotherapy. We have done this in part to respond to a movement within the church which has tried to minimize the differences between these two ministries, on the one hand, and discount the value of Christian psychotherapy, on the other.

In highlighting the differences between psychotherapy and spiritual direction, however, we have not yet answered some compelling questions:

- What is the relationship between spiritual direction and psychotherapy, especially a Christian-based psychotherapy?
- Can people be both in therapy and spiritual direction at the same time, or does the one get in the way of the other?
- Can a counselor provide both spiritual and psychological help at the same time?
- In the final analysis does it really matter to whom you go if you have problems that you have been unable to solve?

We will answer these questions here.

The Case of Trevor

To answer these questions let us consider a typical case of a man named Trevor. He is a twenty-four-year-old unmarried graphic artist who went to see his pastor because he felt unhappy, dissatisfied, and despondent about his life. He no longer dated and complained of poor self-esteem. As he told his pastor how he felt, Trevor wept. He reported that he met weekly with a small prayer group and tried to pray on his own but found his prayers to be dry, even depressing. He no longer felt close to God.

His pastor knew that Trevor needed help, but what kind? Trevor seemed to be going through a depression, but he also kept talking about his problems in spiritual terms. So should his pastor refer Trevor to a psychologist or to a spiritual director?

Playing It Safe

In Trevor's case the pastor decided to play it safe and put Trevor in touch with both a spiritual director and a psychologist. Trevor agreed and over the next few months found both to be very helpful, although for very different reasons.

One of the first exercises that Trevor's spiritual director had him do was to write a "spiritual autobiography." Trevor also began to keep a daily journal of his thoughts and feelings about God and how God was working in his life. These exercises gave him a chance to ponder again the wonderful ways God moved in his life.

In discussing his spiritual autobiography, Trevor also discovered that he felt drawn to a new challenge—working with those in physical pain and crisis. He began volunteering to visit church members who were in the hospital. Some were terminally ill; others were facing the prospect of surgery. Through his own spiritual direction, Trevor developed a deep understanding of how God's comfort could help in times of trouble, and he grew very effective in ministering to others.

The Role of Prayer in Spiritual Direction

Trevor's spiritual director also talked a great deal with Trevor about his prayer life. Trevor had been trying, with very little success, to memorize Bible verses ever since he was in elementary school. His prayer life consisted of trying to repeat as many Bible verses as he could remember. As he became more and more depressed, he continued this type of prayer and crammed his mind with verses to memorize. Needless to say, he found it so difficult that he began to dislike praying and rarely even picked up his Bible anymore.

His spiritual director suggested that he stop trying to memorize verses and instead use a different technique: He was to imagine that Jesus was with him constantly. When he was sitting, Jesus was sitting beside him. When he got up to walk, Jesus was walking with him. He was to imagine that Jesus was talking not only to the disciples but to him also, and asking him to respond.

Trevor found this exercise easy to do and became very excited about this alternative form of prayer! It helped him to break out of the meaningless habits he had developed over the years. By thinking of prayer simply as "conversations with God" and using his imagination to involve his whole being, he had found a way to rejuvenate his prayer life.

After the first few months of regular meetings with his spiritual director, Trevor decided to reduce the frequency of their meetings to about once every six weeks. These less frequent meetings were sufficient to nurture his spiritual life and maintain his new-found spirituality. They also helped him discern if God was calling him to change careers. Since he had discovered how well he could work with seriously ill people, he was seriously considering changing careers so that he could work with people in hospitals.

Trevor's Psychotherapy

Trevor's experience with the psychologist, though extremely helpful and necessary for his total healing, was quite different. The psychologist began by conducting a thorough evaluation of Trevor's personality and emotional functioning. He administered several assessment and diagnostic tests, and the results showed that Trevor's depression was not the kind that would respond to medication. His depression was a "reactive" depression, and it was not likely that he would harm himself. Instead, the personality tests revealed that

Trevor had a strong tendency to keep to himself when under stress. This is sometimes called an "introverted" personality style.

But the tests also revealed a more serious problem. A careful evaluation of Trevor's thinking and reasoning skills showed that while Trevor had very strong non-verbal skills, such as puzzle-solving and designing, he suffered from a significant deficiency in his ability to read and write. While Trevor was totally surprised to discover this weakness, the psychologist was not. Such deficiencies are found in a small percentage of the population even when their intelligence is quite high. People who have not learned how to work with this deficiency tend to experience a fair amount of unexplainable failure, especially in the work setting. Persons with this deficiency often develop a high level of frustration, get angry easily, and have a low tolerance for criticism.

Healing Through Therapy

As Trevor and his therapist started working together, they were able to identify some of the reasons why he became frustrated so easily. While he loved his work as an artist, he had been increasingly asked to do work of a highly technical nature. Not only did he have to prepare complex technical drawings, but he also had to add descriptive text. What he produced was not good enough for his boss, who began to put increased pressure on Trevor.

This pressure had a downward spiral effect. The more his boss pressured him, the less effective Trevor was in understanding the complex technical aspects of what he was to produce. He began to feel panic every time his boss gave him a new assignment. The harder he tried, the worse it seemed to get!

This psychologist helped Trevor to understand how his reading and writing deficiency had made it difficult for him to comprehend what he was to do. Trevor also saw how his introverted personality style caused him to lose the support of his friends in stressful times, which made things even worse.

Trevor also became aware that as a child he was frequently teased and called "dummy." The psychologist helped Trevor to connect these early experiences to his current work problems. Trevor felt as if his boss were continually calling him "dummy," even though his boss never used that word.

Trevor learned and practiced some assertiveness skills with his psychologist and was able to explain his difficulty to his boss. Slowly his confidence came back, and he increased his ability to ask clarifying questions to ensure he understood directions. He explained to his boss that he wanted to focus his energy on his graphic work, where his strength lay. Someone else could do the writing better than he could. By decreasing the amount of writing he had to do, he could spend more time designing and drawing, which was where his real talent was.

Trevor was surprised to find that once his boss understood his deficiencies, he became very supportive. He was happy to allow Trevor to spend more time doing what he did best.

At this point, then, Trevor's work with his spiritual director converged with his psychotherapy to produce a harmonized outcome. Both his spiritual and his psychological healing intersected and reinforced each other.

The Collaboration Between Psychotherapy and Spiritual Direction

We tell Trevor's story not just because it points out the marked differences between spiritual direction and psychotherapy, but because it demonstrates how they can potentially work together.

At first glance the processes used by the psychotherapist and the spiritual director are strikingly similar. Both professionals wanted to help Trevor become a healthier and happier person. With both he talked about his thoughts, feelings, and behaviors, and worked on how to bring his internal world into harmony with his external world. He even talked about both spiritual and psychological matters with both of them. This demonstrates that it is not possible to ignore spiritual matters in psychotherapy, just as it isn't possible to ignore psychological matters in spiritual direction. We cannot completely compartmentalize the human person!

Despite these similarities in the early stages of his encounter with each professional, Trevor's experience with the psychologist was very different from his experience with the spiritual director. These differences became evident right from the first session. While both the psychologist and spiritual director were interested in evaluating Trevor's problems, they were each looking at these problems from a different perspective and evaluating different aspects of the problem. The psychologist relied primarily on scientific clinical assessment tools, while the spiritual director used primarily spiritual discernment.

This difference in methods of evaluation is worthy of special note here. We accept that "discernment" is necessary from a spiritual director. The work is spiritual in nature, so it is natural to expect that the Holy Spirit will be invoked in helping with the evaluation process in spiritual formation. But a psychologist cannot depend solely on any form of psychological discernment. Certainly, as a Christian, a psychologist is just as open to the promptings of the Holy Spirit, but psychological diagnosis must depend heavily on empirically derived tests, not intuitive feelings.

The best way to understand this is to consider the work of the Christian physician. He or she may be very open to any wisdom God imparts, but a physician must still run blood tests, take a pulse, record an EKG, and the like. Any physician who neglects standard medical testing and treatment, no matter how devoted to God, is guilty of negligence. That is what he or she is being paid to do!

This is not to say that with experience, a psychologist, as with a physician, doesn't come to develop intuitive feelings about the nature of human problems. We do! I (Dr. Hart) can "feel" a severe depression right from the moment I first set eyes on the patient, even though I cannot always explain why I get the feeling. It comes with lots of experience in treating depression. But I have to go well beyond my intuition and use objective assessment devices to confirm these feelings if I am going to act professionally.

In Trevor's case, the differences between the approach of his spiritual director and his psychologist became even more obvious once the evaluation phase was finished and both began treating Trevor. His spiritual director continued to focus on Trevor's experience of God—within him, in his world, and in his prayer life. His psychologist, on the other hand, kept his focus on Trevor's awareness of his thoughts, feelings, and behaviors.

The Science of Psychology Versus the Art of Spiritual Direction

The psychologist and spiritual director had different standards in mind as they tried to figure out what would be the best and most reliable way to help Trevor. The psychologist focused on testing and treating Trevor in a way that had scientific integrity.

Trevor's spiritual director, on the other hand, engaged in discerning the work of God in Trevor's life. To do this the spiritual director helped Trevor to think about how his upbringing, personality, and level of maturity were limiting his experience of God. The criteria he was using had nothing to do with scientific standards. Rather, the spiritual director's frame of reference was Scripture and the tradition of Christian spirituality.

Both the psychologist and the spiritual director were interested in helping Trevor find more meaning in his life. They helped Trevor interpret the events of his life in a new way which was closer to reality. However, while his psychologist limited his version of reality to what he had discovered from his tests and interviews, the spiritual director was able to help Trevor reinterpret his circumstances in light of the work of the Holy Spirit. These different interpretations are not in opposition but complement each other.

While psychology and spiritual direction are complementary, they are also two different disciplines. They have different histories, different goals, different techniques, and different accountability standards. Training is provided in different departments in seminaries and universities, and two different communities hold each practitioner accountable for the quality of their work. A summary of the important differences between spiritual direction and psychology can be found in the table on the following page.

	SPIRITUAL DIRECTION	PSYCHOTHERAPY
Goal	Increase person's awareness of God in life circumstances, in "internal world," and in prayer life.	Assess strengths and weaknesses in thoughts, feelings, behaviors, and relationships, and facilitate healing in these.
Initial Assessment	Discern the work of God. Discover the call of God behind the problem. Improve the general health of prayerful relationship with God.	Understand and clarify thinking skills, assumptions, feelings, and personality; clarify roots of problem in history, family issues, etc.
Techniques Used	Interview and dialogue, spiritual autobiography, journaling; possibly questionnaires, such as the Myers-Briggs.	Interview, dialogue; scientific assessment of thinking strengths and weaknesses. Measurement of thoughts; measurement of personality.
Content of Sessions	Feelings, thoughts, impulses, desires, experiences; intuitions, dreams; both "psychological" and "spiritual."	Feelings, thoughts, impulses, desires, experiences; both "psychological" and "spiritual."
Training of Professional	Holy Scripture, theology, Christian spirituality, basic counseling/listening skills.	Scientific evaluation of human qualities. Proper use of validated treatments.
Personal Qualities Needed	Spiritual gift of discernment; interpersonal sensitivity, committed personal and communal prayer life, "basic" mental health.	Interpersonal sensitivity. Appropriate value commitments, substantial mental health.

Integration?

Over the past several years many in the church have attempted to integrate elements of spiritual direction and psychology. In fact, the argument for this integration makes a great deal of sense. We at the Graduate School of Psychology of Fuller Theological Seminary work hard to achieve as much integration as possible between the disciplines of psychology and spiritual formation. All our students take extensive course work in theology while they work on their own therapy and development as marriage therapists or clinical psychologists.

The work of the Christian psychologist is incomplete without the discernment of the Holy Spirit, and the work of the spiritual director is greatly enhanced by the insights of psychologists. How anyone can believe that you can leave the psychological dimensions of the human person "outside" while you work on spiritual matters "inside" is beyond belief! Yet many well-meaning Christian leaders adamantly assert that psychology must be kept out of the spiritual formation formula.

Some have proposed that psychology and spiritual formation should be combined to form a new type of counselor. They suggest that spiritual and psychological matters are not really separable and should therefore be treated together. You might have heard of some of these psychological ministries. They use names like "psycho-spirituality," "biblical counseling," "Christotherapy," and even "spiritual psychology." While it is not our purpose to decry such ministries here, we do want to emphasize that there is a limit to which these disciplines can be combined, beyond which no one is doing justice to either.

First let us note the obvious benefits and blessings we have seen when these two disciplines are brought together. Clearly, the field of Christian psychology has been made aware of how prayer styles can differ, how spirituality can take many forms, and how the Holy Spirit works in the healing of the emotions. A close interaction with spiritual direction has also helped psychologists to know when they should refer patients to spiritual directors for specific work on spiritual matters. Some of us have even learned how to stay out of the way of the Spirit's work!

Spiritual directors, on the other hand, have learned a great deal about how psychological factors can both help and hinder spiritual direction. In particular, spiritual directors have learned a great deal from psychologists about the physical causes of mood problems, how to sort through confusing interpersonal dynamics, how early life trauma can inhibit spirituality later in life, and how to improve their listening skills. As a matter of fact, most spiritual directors now typically receive psychological training as part of their preparation for spiritual formation. This has helped them to be more effective in relating to people.

But too much coordination of the two disciplines, especially when one person tries to do both, is fraught with problems. The most obvious danger is the tendency to psychologize spiritual direction. *A Code of Ethics for Spiritual Directors* warns that "wise spiritual directors continually remind themselves of the purpose of spiritual direction and of how easily it can slide into the style of counseling."[1]

The danger here is quite obvious and serious. When spiritual directors get lost in psychotherapy-land, they are not likely to be effective spiritual guides and might even end up doing a significant amount of harm.

Mistakes are also possible when psychologists rely upon spiritual direction techniques to the neglect of their training in psychology. These mistakes are typically made by well-meaning psychologists who wish to increase the trust of their clients by dealing with their spiritual sensitivities. The difficulty, of course, arises when the dynamics of faith are not appropriately understood by the psychologist.

In addition, very few people have the appropriate gifts, training, and background to do both psychotherapy and spiritual direction. The most dangerous situation comes from someone who is trained in one of these disciplines trying to do the other. Remember the old adage that "a little bit of knowledge is a dangerous thing"? Anyone who is combining psychotherapy and spiritual direction is walking a tightrope. Not that it cannot be done, but it takes a very unique person with some very special training to do justice to both. Doing it well requires both special gifts and ongoing supervision and training in both. We would suggest that unless you absolutely trust someone who claims to be able to do both, you should seek out a specialist in each field.

Choosing One or the Other

This brings us back to a question most commonly asked by those seeking help: "How do you know whether to see a spiritual director or a psychotherapist?" The answer can be summarized in five straightforward rules:

Rule #1

If your problem is causing significant psychological symptoms, such as anxiety or depression, or if it has been plaguing you more than nine months, or if it has caused your work or relationships to suffer, then you should see a good psychologist who can properly evaluate you. You can always handle spiritual direction after you have a good handle on the nature of your problem.

Rule #2

If you have health problems with your soul (i.e., problems praying, problems participating in Christian community, etc.) which started first, or if these problems are your primary concern, see a spiritual director first.

Rule #3

It is acceptable and often a good idea to go to both a spiritual director *and* a psychotherapist during some periods of life.

Rule #4

You do not need to be in crisis to benefit from spiritual direction or psychotherapy; both offer an opportunity to live with more freedom, love, and effectiveness.

Rule #5

If you cannot decide what kind of help you need or want, interview both spiritual directors and psychotherapists and choose the *person* you feel most comfortable with. You can always change your mind down the road.

Appendix A

Professional and Certifying Organizations

American Counseling Association
5999 Stevenson Ave.
Alexandria, VA 22304–3300

ACA is a professional interest group with several divisions. It does not certify members.

American Association for Marriage and Family Therapy
1100 17th Street N.W.
The 10th Floor
Washington, D.C. 20036–4601
(202) 452–0109

AAMFT does accredit programs but does not certify members.

American Association of Christian Counselors
P.O. Box 739
Forest, VA 24551
(800) 526–8673

AACC is a professional interest group that does not accredit programs or certify members.

American Association of Pastoral Counselors
9504A Lee Highway
Fairfax, VA 22031–2303

AAPC offers certification to members.

American Mental Health Counselors Association
5999 Stevenson Avenue
Alexandria, VA 22304

American Nurses Association
600 Maryland Avenue, Ste. 100
Washington, D.C. 20024
(800) 284–2378

Psychiatric nurses can receive certification. However, to check on a nurse's certification status, you will need a signed consent form from the nurse in question and $10.

American Psychiatric Association
1400 K Street, N.W.
Washington, DC 20005

American Psychological Association
750 First Street, NE
Washington, D.C. 20002

The APA is the primary accrediting organization for schools that teach psychology, and the primary professional organization for psychologists.

Christian Association for Psychological Studies
P.O. Box 310400
New Braunfels, TX 78131–0400

CAPS is a professional organization with a code of ethics that members are asked to endorse.

National Association of Social Workers
750 First Street N.E., Ste. 700
Washington, DC 20002

NASW keeps track of those certified in the the Academy of Certified Social Workers (ACSW).

National Board for Certified Counselors, Inc.
3-D Terrace Way
Greensboro, NC 27403
(910) 547–0607

NBCC offers certification to members, and can tell you which members are in good standing.

Recommended Reading List

Aftel, M. and R. T. Lakoff, R. T. *When Talk is Not Cheap: Or, How to Find the Right Therapist When You Don't Know Where to Begin.* New York: Warner, 1985.

Anderson, R. S. *Christians Who Counsel: The Vocation of Holistic Therapy.* Grand Rapids: Zondervan, 1992.

Barry, W. A. and W. J. Connolly. *The Practice of Spiritual Direction.* New York: Seabury, 1983.

Ehrenberg, O. and E. Ehrenberg. *The Psychotherapy Maze: A Consumer's Guide to Getting In and Out of Therapy.* New York: Simon and Schuster, 1986.

Fischer, S. T. *Choosing a Psychotherapist: A Consumer's Guide to Mental Health Treatment.* Clarkston: Minerva, 1986.

Gold, M. *When Someone You Love Is in Psychotherapy.* Alameda: Hunter House, 1993.

Groeschel, B. J. *Spiritual Passages.* New York: Crossroad, 1983.

Hagberg, J. O. and R. A. Guelich. *The Critical Journey: Stages in the Life of Faith.* Dallas: Word Publishing, 1989.

Hart, A. D. *Me, Myself, and I: How Far Should We Go in Our Search for Self-fulfillment?* Ann Arbor: Servant, 1992.

Jones, A. W. *Exploring Spiritual Direction: An Essay on Christian Friendship.* New York: Seabury, 1982.

Kelsey, M. *Christianity as Psychology.* Minneapolis: Augsburg, 1986.

Laplace, J. *Preparing for Spiritual Direction.* Chicago: Franciscan Herald Press, 1975.

Leech, K. *Soul Friend: An Invitation to Spiritual Direction.* New York: HarperCollins, 1992.

May, G. G. *Care of Mind, Care of Spirit: A Psychiatrist Explores Spiritual Direction.* New York: HarperCollins, 1992.

Neimark, P. *Same Time Next Week? How to Leave Your Therapist.* Westport, CT. Arlington House, 1981.

Peterson, E. H. *The Contemplative Pastor: Returning to the Art of Spiritual Direction.* Grand Rapids: Eerdmans, 1989.

Striano, J. *How to Find a Good Psychotherapist: A Consumer Guide.* Santa Barbara: Professional, 1987.

Notes

Chapter 2
Obstacles to Finding the Help You Need

1. Stanton L. Jones, "A Constructive Relationship for Religion with the Science and Profession of Psychology: Perhaps the Boldest Model Yet," *American Psychologist* 49, no. 3, 194–99. Dr. Jones, a professor of psychology at Wheaton College, provides a helpful and brief summary of this problem.

Chapter 4
Psychology in the Formation of Christian Character

1. Many people would also include humanistic psychotherapy as a fifth strategy to help people change. We have chosen not to include it here in light of the unique contradictions it presents to Christian theology. See Dr. Hart's book *Me, Myself, and I* (Ann Arbor, Mich.: Servant, 19??).

Chapter 9
Spiritual Direction in the Formation of Christian Character

1. William Barry and William Connolly, *The Practice of Spiritual Direction*. New York: Seabury, 8.

2. Will Durant, *The Story of Civilization: The Age of Faith*. New York: Simon and Schuster, 1950, 958–83, gives an interesting summary of this period in the church.

Chapter 12
Psychology and Spiritual Direction:
Bringing the Two Together

1. T. M. Hedberg and B. Caprio, *A Code of Ethics for Spritual Directors*. Pecos: Dove, 1992.